PRAISE FOR OPEN REALITY

This is a book about possibility and hope—so much needed—as we go forward uniting humanity to survive, while learning to live in harmony with ourselves and Nature, our life-supporting environment in a holistic world.

—ALLAN SAVORY, ECOLOGIST AND PRESIDENT,
SAVORY INSTITUTE & SAVORY GLOBAL

This brave and important book has found its way into our hands and our hearts just in time. Please read. We need the wisdom of Shodo's deep practice and insight in the times we are facing. A must read today.

—ROSHI JOAN HALIFAX, ABBOT, UPAYA ZEN CENTER
AND THE AUTHOR OF MANY BOOKS, INCLUDING
STANDING AT THE EDGE, BEING WITH DYING,
AND THE FRUITFUL DARKNESS

Shodo Spring invites us to reshape reality—not by deploying AI and carbon nanofibers, but by nurturing our deep roots in nature and Indigenous wisdom. This book can help us awaken from the nightmare that is modern industrial life; every chapter is a not-so-gentle nudge.

—RICHARD HEINBERG, AUTHOR OF
POWER: LIMITS AND PROSPECTS FOR HUMAN SURVIVAL,
THE END OF GROWTH, AND OTHER BOOKS

This book of beautiful, contemplative reflections offers keen insights into the deep, underlying roots of the convoluted network of crises we face both as individuals and as members of a single global community. The path out of our impasse, out of this overwhelming "polycrisis," Shodo argues, does not lie in more sophisticated technologies or more finely tuned policies but in a recognition of our kinship with—indeed, our identity with—the totality of life on this planet and the entire ever-unfolding mystery of the cosmos. She proposes not only theoretical principles to guide us, but also practical exercises to literally return us to our senses.

—*Ven. Bhikkhu Bodhi, Buddhist scholar and the author and translator of many books*

The gift of the author's beautifully articulated vision and guiding voice helps us to imagine, understand, and remember—even in this techno-industrial age—how we may take our place together with all living things, so that life's joyful and miraculous way may be maintained. Unwrap this gift, open it up, and see.

—*Peter Levitt, author, translator, and editor of many books, including* Fingerpainting on the Moon, Yin Mountain, *and* The Essential Dogen

Open Reality offers a credible antidote to the despair that deflates our creative powers and disconnects us from each other. It reminds us of who humans are, have been, and can be again, and imagines a respectful loving and working relationship with the other beings who share this earth.

—*Kritee Kanko, Climate scientist, Zen Teacher and Cofounder of Boundless in Motion*

Open Reality offers us an open-hearted and unflinching challenge: get into right relationship with everything. Somehow this book looks backwards, forwards, and directly at the present all at once. It is a warm invitation into the hope, practice, and possibility of radical ecological transformation.

—BEN CONNELLY, ZEN PRIEST AND AUTHOR OF
INSIDE THE GRASS HUT,
MINDFULNESS AND INTIMACY, AND OTHER BOOKS

With spare and simple language, Shodo Spring addresses the fact that "something is waking up in us." Shodo's easy prose acknowledges the generational traumas of civilizations genocides for perpetrators and victims alike. Refraining from blame and shame, *Open Reality* gathers together tools from Buddhist, Indigenous, and scientific practice to ask new questions about old problems.

—COURTNEY WORK, ASSOCIATE PROFESSOR OF
ETHNOLOGY, NATIONAL CHENGCHI UNIVERSITY,
AND AUTHOR OF TIDES OF EMPIRE

Shodo Spring's *Open Reality* invites the reader to respond internally and through relationships to the unraveling of civilization and its unsustainable complexities. Hopeful and deeply pragmatic, she shares insights from her Zen practice as an ordained priest, from her community activism, and from the land which sustains her.

—PETER BANE, FOUNDER/PUBLISHER OF
PERMACULTURE DESIGN magazine, AUTHOR OF
THE PERMACULTURE HANDBOOK:
GARDEN FARMING FOR TOWN AND COUNTRY, AND
EXECUTIVE DIRECTOR OF
THE PERMACULTURE INSTITUTE OF NORTH AMERICA

My thanks to Shodo for the thoughtful reflections on how we might go where we need to go. To read them is to walk together through the polycrisis with a compassionate spiritual friend.

—DAVID LOY, AUTHOR OF ECODHARMA:
BUDDHIST TEACHINGS FOR THE ECOLOGICAL CRISIS
AND MANY OTHER BOOKS

If we are the least bit aware of the degradation of our shared home—planet Earth—then we might be stuffing or projecting that fear somewhere. How might we use our emotions more productively for a life of joy and life-giving interconnectivity? Zen priest Shodo Spring, in communion with non-human and human beings, interprets the wisdom of the beings and the ages for those of us who have forgotten that we know how to live peaceably with Earth's inhabitants.

—PAMELA AYO YETUNDE, AUTHOR OF
CASTING INDRAS NET:
FOSTERING SPIRITUAL KINSHIP AND COMMUNITY

True practice is not work, not even seeking enlightenment, but playing freely. Shodo's book brings this essential teaching into the reality of todays world, using history and stories to help us change our own framework from work to play, even in crisis.

—SHOHAKU OKUMURA, AUTHOR, TRANSLATOR,
AND EDITOR OF MANY BOOKS, INCLUDING
LIVING BY VOW *AND* THE MOUNTAINS AND WATERS SUTRA

OPEN
REALITY

MEETING THE POLYCRISIS
TOGETHER WITH ALL BEINGS

SHODO SPRING

Sea Crow Press

Copyright © 2025 by Shodo Spring
Open Reality: Meeting the Polycrisis Together With All Beings

All rights reserved.
No part of this book may be reproduced in any form or by any electronic or mechanical means, including information storage and retrieval systems, without written permission from the author, except for the use of brief quotations in a book review.

Published 2025
Sea Crow Press LLC
www.seacrowpress.com
Barnstable, MA 02630 USA

First Edition

PRINT ISBN: 978-1-961864-30-6
E-ISBN: 978-1-961864-31-3
Library of Congress Control Number: 2025933424

Cover Image: ID 346295877 © Khoirul Anwar | Dreamstime.com

CONTENTS

PART 1
LOSING OUR PLACE, AND FINDING IT

1. Refusal Is the Foundation of Sorrow	3
2. Return	9
3. Getting Real	11
Interlude: A New Story	13

PART 2
WE ARE BETTER THAN WE THOUGHT

4. Ancestors	17
5. Who We Are Now	21
6. Systems	23
7. Cost-Benefit Analysis	27
8. Limits	29
9. The Self	31
10. The Great God Pan Is Not Dead	33
11. Trauma Survivors	35
12. How It Works	39
13. Beyond False Hope	47
Interlude: When Everything Is Conscious	51

PART 3
HOW SHALL WE LIVE IN THESE TIMES?

14. Necessity	55
15. Nobody But Us	59
16. Finding the Will	67
17. Values	71
18. Mending Into Life	73
19. Lived by All Beings	77
20. Changing the Structure of Reality	81

Interlude: Sowing Clover 89

PART 4

WHAT WE DO NOW

21. Taking Our Places 93
22. A Promise of Help 97

Afterword: Sacred Practice 101
Appendix 1: Rewriting a History That Is False 105
Appendix 2: True Reports of What People Are Like 111
Life-Affirming Resources 117
Acknowledgments 125
About the Author 127
About the Press 129
Notes 131

This is not a toolbox for protecting life
—others are doing that well elsewhere—
but nourishment for those
who take up the tools and do the work,
throwing our lives into the uncertainty
and creating the future.

POLYCRISIS (NOUN):

- A confluence of multiple, interacting, dangerous trends or events.

- A time of great disagreement, confusion, or suffering caused by multiple problems happening at the same time, which together have profound effects.[1]

---

1. I first learned the word polycrisis in May 2023 during a Kincentric Leadership retreat where Kritee, one of the two facilitators, introduced her trauma- and race-informed definition of this term. Her discussion is at https://www.kriteekanko.com/polycrisis.

PROLOGUE

ALL LIVING THINGS SPEAK US INTO EXISTENCE

It is common to confuse the end of modern civilization with the end of human life, to think it's too late to stop the many crises we face, to forget the lives of other beings. Here, now, we remember those other beings, and consider that something may be more powerful than our own creations.

Our bodies are water, moving with the ocean tides. Our bodies are matter, hungering for the feel of the earth underfoot. Each is a cousin of the microbes in the soil and a relative of the bur oaks up the hill.

I write not about the sixty percent of the human body composed of molecules of water, but of water that moves in the air, flows in and out, rises and swells like ocean tides, flows from high places to low, bubbles over rocks, thunders down from the sky, carves a new path through the soft earth and even through rock. That water is our birth, our home.

Humans have known forever that we are small in a large universe. Only modern humans have imagined ourselves as gods, all-powerful. And only with this fantasy have humans come to the edge of destroying life on earth. Yet we call this the only way to live.

I walk on the morning grass, dew cool against my bare feet, drops hanging on pine needles brushing against my face. My thirsty mouth takes in water from those needles one drop at a time; from a glass it swallows huge gulps of water, cooling, relieving desiccated tissues.

What if there were another way to live, embedded in a world of living, conscious, sacred beings? What if that were the way to save ourselves?

Each body is multitudes. Thirty-nine trillion microbes among thirty trillion cells:[i] that alone must give pause to any dream of independence. More: my body is the frog perching under the leaves of the yellow bean plant. The fly buzzing my head, and my immediate annoyance. The spider thin and graceful in a corner of the bedroom, the other thick and black on the wall of the hallway, moving too fast for me to take it outdoors.

What if, by recovering the deep knowing of our ancestors, we could heal the trauma that we call normal life? What if we could save ourselves, our grandchildren, millions of children and adults right now from starvation, wildfire, drowning, enslavement, from becoming refugees in a barren world?

Once during a days-long meditation retreat, hot and sweating, mind wandering, I found myself grateful for small flies walking across my face, crawling into my ears, bringing me back to now. It was a moment of grace.

It's too much to imagine. Yet, without imagining it, we hurtle ever faster toward disaster.

This body is earth. That actually means vast reaches of space with electrons, atoms, molecules spinning and somehow held together, the mystery of solid matter that is merely bits of energy. I mean to speak of earth, minerals, substance, gravity—what we recognize as home.

What have we got to lose? Well, yes, the entire life that we know; yes, safety, convenience, familiarity. What else? What if we could lose the violence of poverty, end our fear of strangers, stop the epidemic of depression, walk away from addiction, leave behind the utter loneliness of trusting no one?

This body belongs here. The winds blow through, the tides move, the earth holds, and some spark of awareness makes its home in this one body called mine, in these bodies we call ours.

Seeing each other, we create each other. We are no more separate than left hand from right.

PART 1

LOSING OUR PLACE, AND FINDING IT

Life is a planetary level phenomenon and the Earth has been alive for at least 3,000 million years. To me, the human move to take responsibility for the living Earth is laughable—the rhetoric of the powerless. The planet takes care of us, not we of it. Our self-inflated moral imperative to guide a wayward Earth, or heal our sick planet, is evidence of our immense capacity for self-delusion. Rather, we need to protect ourselves from ourselves.

—Lynn Margulis

ONE

REFUSAL IS THE FOUNDATION OF SORROW

The reason we think climate change is hopeless is because we think we're the only ones here.

It's not only our refusal to let go of the comforts of industrial civilization. It's also that we look only for technological solutions. We refuse to work with trees and prairies, wolves and deer, to ask for help from mountains and oceans. We assume they are unconscious and treat them as lifeless objects, even as both science and practice increasingly prove otherwise.[i]

I write to invite you back into that place where we know our home is the earth and our family is the communities of life.

We are mourning. Our bodies are mourning. The whole body of the human species is mourning. You can tell were mourning by the plague; by COVID, by an illness affecting the lungs which are where grief shows itself. As we return to business as usual, anger and fear take the lead. Wars escalate, blaming and scapegoating proliferate, and we form alliances more by whom we fear than by anything else.[ii]

September: a red squirrel chattered in the tree not eight feet away. I looked, she looked back, we looked at each other. She moved a little farther away, looked at me again, then ran off into the woods. No question she felt me looking. I didn't say a word.

3

SHODO SPRING

The first grief beneath all of these is that we don't trust the world in which we live.

Long ago, people trusted the gods, or God, or the spirits, or the plants and animals and mountains and rivers. Since European humanism overthrew an oppressive church, we have to be our own gods.

So we act as gods. We claim the right to use everything, consume anything, build, pave, plow, create. We even create new forms of life through genetic engineering. And "we" are the only ones that matter. When we kill other humans *en masse*, we call it genocide, if we recognize them as human. When we kill animals *en masse,* we call it food production. When we kill forests, prairies, and ecosystems *en masse* we call it development, and applaud ourselves.

Having to be our own gods is the foundational sorrow.

But we are not God, or gods; we are humans with powerful technology, who deny, as a culture, that anything is holy.

Most people in the history of the world have lived a different way.

Robin Wall Kimmerer offers an image from her family, canoe camping in the Adirondacks, not so long ago a home-made way of beginning the day.

> I can picture my father, in his red-checked wool shirt, standing atop the rocks above the lake. When he lifts the coffeepot from the stove the morning bustle stops; we know without being told that it's time to pay attention. ... He pours coffee out on the ground in a thick brown stream.
> The sunlight catches the flow, striping it amber and brown and black as it falls to the earth and steams in the cool morning air. With his face to the morning sun, he pours and speaks into the stillness, "Here's to the gods of Tahawus." ... So begins each morning in the north woods: the words that come before all else. I was pretty sure that no other family I knew began their day like this, but I never questioned the source of those words and my father never explained. They were just part of our life among the lakes. But their rhythm made me feel at home and the ceremony

OPEN REALITY

drew a circle around our family. By those words we said "Here we are," and I imagined that the land heard us and murmured to itself, "Ohh, here are the ones who know how to say thank you." ... "[W]hen I first heard in Oklahoma the sending of thanks to the four directions at the sunrise lodge the offering in the old language of the sacred tobacco I heard it as if in my father's voice. The language was different but the heart was the same. ... It was in the presence of the ancient ceremonies that I understood that our coffee offering was not secondhand, it was ours.[iii]

We, industrial humans, call those other people hunter-gatherers, or pastoralists, or horticulturists, and we think we are better off.

Yet we also picture their way of life in the Garden of Eden: abundant, safe, easy, well-nourished, supported. And you get to walk with God every day.

You get to walk with God every day.

Being thrown out to do agriculture was the natural result of refusing the gifts freely offered, the inevitable consequence of trying to be gods.

Humans had lived well for millennia. Like other top predators, they lived by culling the old and sick from the herds of other animals around them, and from gathering the surplus of plants, while carefully maintaining the well-being of the host population. Like other animals and plants, in case of drought, flood, or blizzard, some of them would die. They did not expect otherwise.

That way of life has been crowded out over the centuries. Yet it's not completely lost. Not only Kimmerer's family recreating it from their bones. Not only in remote places, either. In Wisconsin, the Menominee people have managed a forest for timber products since 1908, supporting their people for over a hundred years.[iv] The forest is healthier now than when they began.

Humans know how to do this.

But industrial culture does not: as a whole we know how to control, not how to engage; how to destroy, not how to grow. This is our great loss, and the reason we mourn.

We do not know how to be part of the family.

In the natural order of things, there is mystery, whether called God or something else. But in our present society, mystery is excluded, known only by a few, and usually not mentioned. We think we must make sense of everything ourselves. If it doesn't work for our cognitive understanding, we call it silly, or inferior, irrational, primitive, superstitious.

Our imagination is gone.

Instead of asking "how can we live differently?" we ask only "how can we protect this civilization as it is now?" Asking only that question dooms us to failure.

To imagine a whole life: that might be the first step, for many people. To imagine a whole community could be a step for people disappointed but not destroyed, people whose lives have given them the ability to love and to work for what they love. These people are among us, like yeast in bread.

Bill Mollison, watching the devastation of his Tasmanian homeland, and inspired by the richness of the rainforest community, co-invented permaculture after giving up on working within the system. Others followed, birthing regenerative agriculture to not just sustain but restore. In forty-five years, they've made a beginning at imitating the millennia-developed workings of the natural world.

Permaculture has a list of official principles.[v] To me they boil down to two: (1) imitate nature, and (2) imitate traditional indigenous people, who know how to listen to nature.

From arctic to jungle to desert, gathering-hunting societies report a world that cares for them, whether in hardship or in ease. Industrial peoples have been trained to trust only our own technology. We can't imagine living in the embrace of the world. That is the deep, unnamed grief of our time and our people.

Before I went to live in the Arctic in an Inupiaq city, I prepared by reading everything I could about the culture. I can't find this quote from a man who lived the old ways, but it's something like this: "This place is abundant. There

OPEN REALITY

is plenty. We lack for nothing." This in a place that looked bare and bleak, flat, with snow ten months of the year and night six of those months.

One day in Noorvik I met with an Inupiaq elder. This exchange stands out in my memory: "Would you want to live that way again?" "No." "Why?" "People had to take care of each other."

In the words of author Daniel Quinn, we have forgotten how to live in the hands of the gods.[vi] We lack the skills to receive their gifts. We lost the skills through technology.

You can hear it in that elder's words. Living in the hands of the gods also means living in each other's hands. In a culture that lives in the present, there is no need for immortality and no need for transcendence.

Buddhist tradition offers this concept: "hungry ghost" refers to a state of excruciating hunger that nothing can satisfy. Industrial civilization is a hungry ghost, and it makes its people into hungry ghosts. Collectively, it devours everything that is not itself, including forests, minerals, other humans, plants of all kinds, oceans, rivers, every community of life, and it is still hungry. It turns all these living things into a strange thing called profit, which creates an illusion of security but does not satisfy hunger.

It does not understand that real security comes from community, from being embedded in a community in which everyone supports everyone else, whether that community is human or not. This is the loss, the deep grief, impossible to recognize from inside this culture.

Ancient people, living close to the earth, had an intimacy with the forces of nature that we can't even imagine. Consider this story from Derrick Jensen in *Dreams*:

> *Years ago the Okanagan Indian writer and activist Jeannette Armstrong went to northern Russia to stay with traditional indigenous peoples there. The people were hungry because the caribou had not shown up. Then one day one of the people in the village who was skilled in these matters declared the caribou were in a valley some distance away. Hunters set off, found the caribou, killed some to eat, and brought back food and skins. Jeannette*

asked the man how he knew where the caribou were, and he responded, "How do you know where your hand is?"[vii]

"How do you know where your hand is?" In my professional work as a counselor and healer, I sometimes help people to know where their hand is. In modern industrial culture, we have to intentionally learn to experience our own bodies, not even to mention experiencing the world as our body as the man in Russia naturally did. It's a kind of poverty that we don't even notice. Its one of the roots of the violence we now experience in America.

TWO
RETURN

*Like smooth water-polished pebbles, set like jewels in a bracelet
at the bottom of the river of the collective human soul, there are
noble and profound human beings whose radiance and value are
unknown even to their closest neighbors ...*

—Martín Prechtel[i]

Noble and profound human beings. The thought makes one glad. We may hope they will rise and move and act, lead, spread through this culture like a yeast, rising, lightening it, making it soft and beautiful and pliable and edible.

Martín follows with this:

Inside each one of us, sitting like a well-worn jewel in the clear-running river of our own soul, present right here today, there is also a deep and noble human being, unknown even to his or her closest neighbor: that more external outer layer of ourselves who has become a personality of the surrounding culture, instead of that true individual, a person indigenous to our own deeper spiritual landscape.

These noble and profound human beings are not someone else. They are not from somewhere else. They are us, ourselves. It is we who have the beauty and power to bring life back to our people.

For a minute, imagine who you might be if you recognized yourself as a child of the universe, a sister or brother of the trees and stars. For an hour, move through your life as such a person. Then a day, a week, a month.

Such imagining is a first step to moving beyond the crimes of your ancestors, your culture, or even your own self. It's a beginning to being able to forgive them and yourself—and that is an opening to being able to move with freedom and power among human beings.

> *Martin: If there are enough of such humans, then collectively real cultures worth living in, cultures that don't depend on scaredness, scarcity, and sarcasm, could actually begin to cultivate themselves into motion. No longer needing someone else's rails, we could get off the siding, the plastic could disappear, the butterflies could be released, the river could light up.*

We can be those people.

THREE
GETTING REAL

I'm not proposing finding alternative energy sources so we can continue living in the same way we do now. I'm not talking about saving capitalism, creating a socialist utopia, becoming hunter-gatherers, or even finding a new paradigm.

Allowing ourselves to be created by the earth includes letting scarcity and death back into our lives. Being spoken by all living things includes recognizing the abundance that is all around us, that is given rather than taken, natural instead of made, wild not cultivated. It means redefining abundance in terms of relationships, small pleasures, free time, space for creativity, and of course enough food and shelter and safety, rather than bigger houses, better cars, and travel.

We do not need the Green New Deal or a carbon-neutral energy source. We need to know our place in the natural world.

That will include having communities that are able and willing to share the commons, to regulate it for the benefit of all, and to cooperate. Humans know how to do all of these, and have done them for a very long time. I'll give examples in Part II.

We can't become hunter-gatherers, and not only because we lack the skills. The number of people on the planet, combined with the degrada-

SHODO SPRING

tion of the natural world, makes it impossible to feed us all in that way. I agree with Morris Berman, who said:

> [W]hat we need is not a dramatic transformation of reality and culture, but simply the willingness to live in this culture and reality as we work on the intelligent repair of present problems, without hype or bombast, and let the future take care of itself. For that future, when it arrives, will have its problems, and we shall have to deal with them. ... There are two things that strike me as integral to hunter-gatherer civilization that we moderns can adopt, though the process of making these things a part of our lives would be a slow and difficult one. The first is the cultivation of silent spaces; the second, the radical acceptance of death. Both of these contribute greatly to the ability to experience paradox.[i]

The last part of this book addresses the question about how to live. What does Life require of us?

INTERLUDE: A NEW STORY

Every day I wonder whether I should be doing something else. And every day, on thinking about it, I remember Ivan Illich's words:

> *Neither revolution nor reformation can ultimately change a society, rather you must tell a new powerful tale, one so persuasive that it sweeps away the old myths and becomes the preferred story, one so inclusive that it gathers all the bits of our past and our present into a coherent whole, one that even shines some light into the future so that we can take the next step... If you want to change a society, then you have to tell an alternative story.*[i]

Of all the actions I could take, including many that are more dramatic or dangerous, changing the story is the most powerful. We are in the process of changing that story collectively. This book is a part of that change.

PART 2

WE ARE BETTER THAN WE THOUGHT

We are talking only to ourselves.
We are not talking to the rivers, we are not listening to the wind
and stars.
We have broken the great conversation.
By breaking that conversation we have shattered the universe.
All the disasters that are happening now are a consequence of
that spiritual "autism."

—*Thomas Berry*

Part II is about changing a common assumption about what human beings are. Increasingly, archaeology and anthropology refute the idea that humans are inherently selfish and thoughtless, and offer true histories to inform our next creation.

FOUR
ANCESTORS

We did not think of the great open plains, the beautiful rolling hills, and the winding streams with tangled growth as "wild." Only to the White man was nature a "wilderness" and only to him was the land infested by "wild" animals and "savage" people. To us it was tame. Earth was bountiful and we were surrounded with the blessings of the Great Mystery. Not until the hairy man from the east came and with brutal frenzy heaped injustices upon us and the families we loved was it "wild" for us.

—Luther Standing Bear, *Land of the Spotted Eagle*[i]

Here is our usual story about the ancestors.

Stone Age peoples lived in small bands, wild and free, with almost no possessions, children of earth and sky, living from day to day. (Standing Bear speaks from that life, which lasted in much of North America until the European invasion.) For whatever reason they developed agriculture, private property, slavery, and war, and lost their spiritual connection with nature. Then followed a few millennia of valley-based agricultural kingdoms, co-existing uneasily with barbarians in the wilderness, gradually developing more power for the kingdoms, which were complex, unequal, patriarchal, and warlike. Eventually we reached commerce, capitalism, democracy, and then the Industrial Revolution which is "better" even though it vastly widens the gap between the poorest and the wealthy.

Implied and occasionally stated: only simple people can be egalitarian, or only poor people.

And whether egalitarian is good, as Rousseau imagined, or bad, as Hobbes thought, it is no longer available to us, because we're too smart and too rich.

Also implied: there was no other way this could have turned out.

The early hunter-gatherers, or gatherer-hunters, seem to have been pretty egalitarian. They were also more diverse than we commonly imagine.

We know that some of them lived in small bands of twenty or so people, gathering just what they needed for today, and moving often. Because they traveled all the time, they met other people; over the course of time an individual might well have a thousand acquaintances. But there was plenty of space you could go away; you could even go on walkabout for months at a time.

You, together with your band, depended on the world around you for food on a daily basis. If one got food, everyone ate. If there was not food here, you walked to another spot; if there was not food today, probably there would be tomorrow. The world was friendly. "Why should we plant when there are so many mongongo nuts in the world?"[ii]

Hunter-gatherers relied on thousands of kinds of plants and animals. They gathered their food from what grew around them, animals and insects as well as plants and fungi. They moved on when food ran out or the season changed. They fiercely restricted reproduction. They tinkered with the lands around them, modifying waters, planting some of their favorite foods, making the space even more friendly.[iii]

They took what they needed. They tended to ask for help whether from ancestral spirits, sky spirits, the spirits of the animals and plants, or whatever for food, water, warmth, shelter, and safety.

OPEN REALITY

They lived in the present, always alert for opportunity or danger. They didn't store up food or belongings that would be inconvenient for travel. They shared with those around them, knowing others would equally share with them. They traveled to more abundant places as needed, perhaps with the seasons. They could figure on not being hungry for more than a day or two before finding food again.

Anthropologist James Woodburn, studying the Hadza in Tanzania, the San Bushmen and Mbuti Pygmies in Africa, the Pandaram of south India and Batek of Malaysia, noted that they extended equality to gender relations and to different ages. "All such behaviour," Woodburn insisted, "is based on a self-conscious ethos, that no one should ever be in a relation of ongoing dependency to anybody else."[iv] In short, a lot of societies have consciously created egalitarian societies with actual personal freedom for everyone. People can be culturally creative.

There were societies that alternated this kind of small-band roaming with large gatherings that included hierarchy, police, and ritual. Some of these societies made sure the hierarchies did not become permanent. This year's ceremonial rulers would not take the same role next year; there would not be a lasting ruler.[v]

There are also many examples of ancient cities that lack the hierarchy we expect in cities. The arrangement of the buildings, the lack of palaces, the hundreds of similar modest comfortable homes, the existence of large spaces that could be used for public gathering these suggest egalitarian life. Some also show strong evidence of female leadership, respect for women, or equality of rights and freedoms.

Our ancestors were able to treat each other fairly and equally, whether they lived in small bands or large communities. People also do it now; the appendix includes discussion of utopian communities through the past millennium. Humans can do this. Conditions may interfere, including conditions of scarcity and of population pressure. Humans have known how to control their populations, but currently are under great pressure to increase in order for their own group to be more powerful. Thus we consume our children's future. One is reminded of "eating the seed corn," traditionally forbidden unless starvation was imminent, because it destroys the future.

19

This matters. If we think the most advanced state is totalitarian, there is no hope for us to become a whole people. Having multiple successful examples of fair and equal societies, we can venture to dream and create our own society.

The point is that human beings are capable of living together in a wide variety of ways, including in cities, without war and without great inequality. We've done so in many times and many places, including large-scale societies. The freedom to leave, to disobey, and to change social relationships were present for everyone in them without regard to caste or class. Customs such as hospitality ensured these freedoms were not dependent on wealth.

> *As anyone knows who has spent time in a rural community, or serving on a municipal or parish council of a large city, resolving such inequities might require many hours, possibly days of tedious discussion, but almost always a solution will be arrived at that no one finds entirely unfair.*[vi]

Todays bureaucratic states exchange that process for a quick "everyone the same" approach, often administered by algorithms. They suggest that because of prejudice its impossible for human beings to be fair. But they create a process deeply dissatisfying as it ignores the humanity of those involved, and hides discrimination in the structure of the rules.

FIVE
WHO WE ARE NOW

Stories tell us who we are—fiction, documentaries, autobiographies, all kinds of stories give shape and meaning to what it is to be human. More than facts, stories create our images of ourselves and especially the people around us. Were accustomed to negative stories, but there are others.

The Christmas truce happened in 1914, when the expectation had been that the World War would be "done by Christmas." But there they were, a lot of young men, cold and wet. Something happened.

Some stories say one German began to sing "Stille Nacht," others joined, then English, Scots, and Irish sang back. Soldiers ventured out toward each other, and were not shot. In the morning there were invitations, exchanges of gifts, handshakes, and at least one game of football (soccer) played between enemies. It happened in many places, for a few hours or a few days.

The higher-ups made sure it never happened again. Many of the men there had to be transferred away from the front, unable to kill again.[i]

What are humans like, really? Do we prefer to fight, to steal, to take revenge? Or do we naturally cooperate, show kindness, care for each other, until intimidated or tricked into being otherwise? I'll leave for later the matter of humans in other, gentler societies. In the middle of a culture that glorifies violence and greed, we have documented stories that give the lie to the myth of selfishness.

Rebecca Solnit writes:

> *Decades of meticulous sociological research on behavior in disasters, from the bombings of World War II to floods, tornadoes, earthquakes, and storms across the continent and around the world, have demonstrated this [that people help each other]. But belief lags behind, and often the worst behavior in the wake of a calamity is on the part of those who believe that others will behave savagely ...*[ii]

Disaster, along with moments of social upheaval, is when the shackles of conventional belief and role fall away and the possibilities open up.[iii]

A few such stories are in Appendix 2.

SIX

SYSTEMS

In the same way that a colony of bees will instinctively house its queen in the deepest chambers of the hive, so a complex adaptive system buries its most important operating logic furthest from the forces that can challenge them.

—Alnoor Ladha, Martin Kirk; Kosmos Journal, Spring | Summer 2016

This is important. It means that we don't understand much of what is happening around us. It's hidden in the shape of our language, in what our children are taught about the nature of reality, in things that are never said.

This means two things: first, it means embedding the logic in the deep rules that govern the whole. Not just this national economy or that, this government or that, but the mother system the global operating system.[i]

The writer refers here to a human-made system, called the Corposystem by geneticist Lynn Lamoreux.[ii] Its core rule is to increase capital, which means to convert things, human labor, trees, cows, mountains, soils, and water into currency, money—symbols that you cannot eat, wear, or

SHODO SPRING

shelter under, but can probably exchange for those practical needs under rules controlled by state or lord.

In contrast, the core rule of the Biosystem is sustainability, which requires collaborative balance in the long run.

> *And second, it means making these rules feel as intractable and inevitable as possible.*[iii]

The Biosystem, referring here to the whole of life on Earth, is a complex naturally evolved system. It too seeks to continue its existence. The Biosystem thrives with multiple species interacting with each other in ways that continue multiplicity, generate new forms of life, and maintain balance. Monocultures do not function well, and they tend to die out unless artificially supported. The Biosystem requires "a very intricate, balanced communication of information among all its subsystems to sustain that balance."[iv]

An individual species, such as *Homo sapiens*, is also a complex naturally evolved system, and it naturally creates many copies of its DNA. However, no species can live alone; all rely on thousands or millions of other species. Here's an example about the importance of top predators, in Yellowstone National Park.

Humans and wolves were both hunting elk. With elk herds diminished, the wolves turned to livestock, and the humans turned to exterminating wolves. This is how it went:

> *In the 70 years of the wolves absence, the entire Yellowstone ecosystem had fallen out of balance. Coyotes ran rampant, and the elk population exploded, overgrazing willows and aspens. Without those trees, songbirds began to decline, beavers could no longer build their dams and riverbanks started to erode. Without beaver dams and the shade from trees and other plants, water temperatures were too high for cold-water fish.*[v]

This had happened because humans as top predators were out of touch with the natural communities there. It might have been different if the indigenous people had been able to stay and to use their centuries of

OPEN REALITY

experience living harmoniously with that natural community.[vi] Still, the National Park Service eventually recognized a problem, reinstated wolves in 1995, and reported a rebound of life of all kinds.

Top predators are necessary, AND they must follow rules of the Biosystem, including not destroying the last of their prey.

Humans living traditionally have known how to deal with the limits of their environment, including not killing the last fish or harvesting every single wild leek. This is basic for foragers and small farmers. Their understanding is practical, and the consequences are quick. Yet we now live in a culture that neither understands our dependence on those we eat nor lives in practical response to this reality. Industrial humanity is a top predator that doesn't understand its dependence on the others.

Consider this thought: "All beings are the genetic material of the Biosystem."[vii] Complexity makes for stability; every extinction impoverishes the whole. Civilized human history starting with agriculture replaces wild plant and animal biomass with humans, domesticated animals, and monocrops. Where there were once hundreds of varieties of sheep, each well adapted to a particular place, now there are a few. This makes the whole system fragile. Whales enrich the world's oceans enormously; they have been depleted first by whaling, then by the U.S. Navy's sonar, and now by the "Internet of Underwater Things." Beavers are treated as pests now that the fashion for beaver hats has gone, but people are starting to notice that bringing beavers back is a way to repair a river system.

In species we breed for our use—apples, corn, etc.—civilized humans select for the "best" one, and then we breed that one alone.[viii] "Best" is defined as easy to grow in industrial agriculture conditions, and tolerant of shipping and long waits for market. It has little to do with flavor or nutrition, and certainly not long-term ecosystem services. When we do this, we simplify the local Biosystem. It becomes more fragile, more vulnerable to pests and diseases, and less able to recover from disasters. As we reduce the complexity of the gene pool, we have less resilience, more susceptibility to diseases, and a general weakening of the whole. Monocropping does this; introducing GMOs[ix] adds to the problem.

25

SHODO SPRING

Many human societies have successfully cooperated with the long-term good of the whole, and survived for centuries or longer. They participate willingly in the workings of the Biosystem. Industrial or agricultural societies prioritize the success of the Corposystem, assuming godlike powers to repair any damage and thus they do damage.

Looking in terms of systems, it becomes clear that it does not help to be angry with an individual, a company, or even a national government: They are not in control. They are driven by the mandates of the Corposystem to grow, to profit, to turn nature into wealth that can be privatized.

However, the mandate of the Biosystem is to live, to flourish and flower in multi-species abundance. The two are not compatible.

SEVEN

COST-BENEFIT ANALYSIS

One might expect "greater good" to refer to things like protecting children, stopping climate change, ending war, and public health. Instead, it seems usually to involve profit, expansion of infrastructure, and destroying homes and forests.[i] "Greater good" means the good of the industrial system, the Corposystem, growth by domination for profit. If only we valued Gross National Happiness instead of Gross National Product.[ii]

Cost-benefit analysis is said to value the "greater good" over harms or benefits to individuals. It is a creation of modern European civilization.

In medieval Europe property laws were rigid: *"sic utere tuo ut alienum non laedas"* ("use your own so as not to injure another"). If your economic activities harmed your neighbor, you were legally responsible for the harm, regardless of any benefits your economic activity might provide to society. Further, your intention was irrelevant, and no excuse would provide defense.

Attorney Joe Guth described this process of change in his 2008 article "Law for the Ecological Age." The present result is that economic activity is assumed beneficial, and is allowed unless convincingly proven to be harmful. External costs such as human or animal health, and environmental or economic damages, are usually ignored. It is common to ignore legal prohibitions as well.[iii]

Previously, there were things that simply would not be done because people got hurt.[iv] With cost-benefit analysis, those things can be done if the "marginal utility" is positive. Also, now, a dozen harmful things can be done if each one, individually, causes a harm valued as less important than the benefit.

One of the current legal battles is to correct that loophole, so that corporate owners could no longer split up their harmful projects into pieces small enough to meet legal limits. Another is "the precautionary principle": rather than having to prove a project dangerous, it must be proven safe. Environmental Impact Statements express this principle, and are commonly ignored, done sloppily, or produced after the project is already begun.

There's a fundamental problem here: the absence of actual ethical values. When these are set aside in any analysis, cost-benefit or otherwise, people are needlessly harmed, at minimum, and too often needlessly killed. Thus it came to be thought that the deaths of dozens of school children do not outweigh the imagined right to unrestricted use of weapons.

EIGHT
LIMITS

The earth is finite. It did not always seem so.

When I was growing up in the 1950s, world maps still had unknown places. The outlines of continents under ice were merely sketched in, shown as dotted lines. The power of fossil fuels seemed unlimited. We imagined settling the moon. And a four-hour drive was a big deal.

For centuries before that, people's personal worlds were small. Ordinary people lived close to home. The cost of travel, even for the wealthy, was time, money, and danger.

Except, of course, for hunter-gatherers—yet they generally did not travel thousands of miles to new worlds.

Oddly, the hunter-gatherers, who strictly limited their fertility and their belongings, experienced an unlimited life in many ways—wandering, roaming, meeting new people—until their lands dwindled due to colonization and settlement. Modern industrial humans, collectively refusing to limit fertility or possessions, constantly struggle with personal limits, with an unfulfilled sense of entitlement that we should be able to go anywhere and have everything.

When I was a college physics student, one of the professors said something like this: "We have an unusual number of students this year trying to invent a perpetual motion machine. Usually that idea has been beaten out of them by the time they get here." The Second Law of Thermodynamics explains how such a thing is impossible, of course. Now a whole society is gambling that we can work around the Second Law by using energy from sun and wind— ignoring the massive damage done by the processes required to gather and manage that energy, just as the fossil fuels people ignored those processes before us.

The only escape from the Second Law is this: Life is an anti-entropic force. A few people in our age are actively working with that fact. I can't explain in brief.

I began by writing about the awareness of limits in the lives of most people, over centuries, living in a relatively small area. It turns out, although gatherers and hunters were keenly aware of limits of food, water, shelter, and space, there was something different in the personal quality of limits. A natural limit, a natural law, is subjectively different from a law made and enforced by a human authority. What do I mean here?

A simple example will do. What if you were walking along a path, and it started to hail, heavily, pounding your body and bruising you? What feelings arise? You may regret not checking the weather, but most of your energy will be directed toward safety and shelter. What if you were walking on the same path and a group of kids starts throwing pebbles at you? Is your response different? Some of us might forget safety and go to fight with the assaulting group. The idea that the harm is willful gives rise to a whole complicated bunch of feelings. And choosing a response, from calming words to returning the violence, can be agonizing for the thoughtful person.

Anger about hail probably only arises if you envision a personalized God who made it happen. Anger about stone-throwing, or mask mandates, or poverty, is related to the thought that somebody is doing this *to me* and *with intention*. That particular misery is absent when the cause is impersonal or when it can be seen as impersonal.

NINE
THE SELF

Ivan Illich proposes that until written language there was no idea of a permanent self. A self would arise in the telling of a story, and be gone again. [i]

I'm reminded of the Buddhist core teaching: There is no abiding self. There is an ephemeral self, that rises in response to conditions and ends again, that is created moment by moment. The self cannot be exterminated or obliterated because it has always been temporary.

It's a match. The natural state of humanity is that the individual self rises and falls as needed. Our fears about losing identity are just fears: There's nothing to lose.

As I write we are engaged in a struggle for the rights of all kinds of groups that have been ignored, suppressed, exploited, enslaved, dehumanized, denied personhood including the rights of animals, and now the rights of rivers, lakes, wild rice, sacred mountains, and more. To defend them in this society, we claim personhood for them. (As of 2022, nature's rights laws exist in 24 countries, at least seven Tribal Nations in the U.S. and Canada, and over 60 cities and counties throughout the United States.[ii]

This is an improvement over claiming ourselves as the only conscious beings, the only **persons**, with everything else as resources for **us**.

SHODO SPRING

Now we have to share. And as the ones with the most power, this is a step in the right direction. But what happens next?

Mel Bazil, a leader in the Wet'suwet'en land defense against TC Energy and the RCMP[iii] says, "We don't have rights. We have responsibilities." It's not about the individual self, but about the whole.

That's the other way available to us.

Some old spiritual traditions simply have no concept of self. Buddhism looks at the self, sees a problem, and offers a path out of the trap.

What we call "self" is a point of awareness, looking out at the whole world, taking in sensory data, making explanations and stories, and finding ways to negotiate the world. That's all a self is. But when "self" is misunderstood as independent and permanent, the whole person organizes to protect and promote it, and the rest of life is sacrificed.

TEN

THE GREAT GOD PAN IS NOT DEAD

Communal joy and ecstasy form a key part of many cultures, binding them together. In *Dancing in the Streets*,[i] Barbara Ehrenreich describes this phenomenon, tracing its existence both around the world and through history and prehistory. Archaeologists find it in cave drawings thousands of years old; anthropologists observe it in many places. Ecstatic practice is a crucial part of community.

In gathering and hunting societies, the things around us are alive in themselves, not a channel for some other meaning.[ii] The world is as it is, and that's okay, regardless of whether I personally live or die. This has been the root of a way of life that survived for millennia without destroying the land base.

That way is still with us, though often remote from daily life in civilization. Modern life looks askance at religions that include ecstatic practices such as speaking in tongues, even when those religions carry names as accepted as Christian. The early years of ecstatic sects such as Quakers, Shakers, Pentecostalists, and Sufis were all marked by religious persecutions. Twentieth-century America saw the return of wild dancing, originally criticized as too sexual by the authorities of the time, then simply accepted as part of the culture. It was the Boomer generation that, instead of switching to classical music as adults, continued to dance wildly when an occasion could be found. How much is a Grateful Dead concert, a Rainbow People gathering, or a Burning Man festival like the ecstatic dancing of the old days? Joseph Campbell, the great mythologist, went to a Grateful Dead concert. He later said:

> *This is more than music, it turns something on in here [the heart]. And what it turns on is life energy. This is Dionysus talking through these kids. ... It doesn't matter what the name of the god is, or whether it's a rock group or a clergy. It's somehow hitting that chord of realization of the unity of God in you all.*[iii]

Now we increasingly incorporate ceremony into political resistance movements. I remember Standing Rock, the dawn songs, morning prayers at the river in freezing cold, forming a base for the civil disobedience that formed the official activism. All was led by indigenous people who never fully accepted the European version of proper behavior, and this time some of the Europeans followed.

Something is waking up in us. Everywhere people are writing about the need for community, for spirit, for traditional and earth-based religious ways, even about the consciousness of plants, animals, rocks and water. Increasingly, cities and states are freeing their waterways, opening long-buried streams to the sky, welcoming life into human places again. In the forty years that I've been watching this, it's gone from a tiny trickle in the desert to a mighty stream threatening to wash away the metaphorical walls of the city.

The Great God Pan—the god of nature and shepherds and the wild—is not dead, but alive and active in our time, beyond the sects where he was hiding out.

This is the movement that may change our course from death to life, from pavement to celebration, from factory farms to gardens, forests, wetlands, and prairies. As we come back to plant our bodies on the earth again, to walk, to dance, to listen, to receive, to flower in the abundance that still remains, we are enlivened, and our increasing liveliness grows the liveliness of the whole.

"They tried to bury us. They did not know we were seeds."[iv]

ELEVEN
TRAUMA SURVIVORS

Trauma in a person, decontextualized over time, looks like personality.
Trauma in a family, decontextualized over time, looks like family traits.
Trauma in a people, decontextualized over time, looks like culture!

—*Resmaa Menakem*[i]

Our collective understanding of what trauma does to individuals is increasing. We know, now, that certain functions of the mind are disabled, undeveloped, or altered.

> *At times, perpetrators consciously and intentionally use these processes to set up internal systems of self-doubt, second guessing, and shame so that the predator is in control through physiological arousal. Core Survival Networks are created in this context and then reinforced through programming and conditioning. One of the reasons why programming is so powerful and difficult to neutralize is because it essentially "hijacks" a persons core values. This creates internal traps of conscience where people feel like they are betraying their core sense of themselves in the world when they are trying to act against programming.*[ii]

Notice this: Trauma makes it harder to extinguish fear. Fear, shame, and self-doubt are useful to predators. These are embedded physiologically, making it harder for the person to reclaim personal values and integrity.

Naomi Klein's 2007 book *Shock Doctrine* discusses the intentional destruction of individual and culture in this way, using natural calamities to create markets and exploit whole populations. The 2002 Adam Curtis documentary *The Century of the Self* dramatizes how public relations was used to turn rational citizens into emotional, self-centered consumers. It begins with Sigmund Freud and his nephew Edward Bernay's, continues through the deliberate creation of consumerism, and finally addresses how the same practices were used to change the political sphere and destroy public discourse.[iii]

Under a Spell

When an entire society has been programmed—in our case, to consume things and experiences to satisfy invented emotional "needs"—that programming includes every individual, and it's very hard for a person to regain an independent mind. Reality is defined by our programming, and powerful forces come to bear on any attempts to change. Resistance tends to take the form of rebellion, rather than actually changing culture. Or movements that think of themselves as resistance actually accept the basic assumptions of the dominant culture. The strongest options exist for people with a cultural or religious memory of living another way and, as I wrote in 2021, these people are being increasingly recognized as leaders of the change.[iv]

How do you move from a dysfunctional system to one that works?

When I was a kid reciting the confession every Sunday morning in church, I never imagined that people outside the church thought the same.[v] But it turns out that members of industrial civilization often also think they are worthless, separate, lonely individuals, without even a god to save them. They consume out of despair, I think.

Even on a strictly material basis, every person's life depends on everything else: other humans, other living beings, air, water, minerals, soils. We are not separate. Individualism is a confusion. And what makes life

OPEN REALITY

worth living is community, connection, intimacy. Only in very narrow parts of the human world are individual wants prioritized over species survival. And individuality thrives in community.

Happiness comes from relationship, not from things. This has been measured and documented, yet within the Corposystem we don't know how to manifest it.[vi] Instead, we live with constant stress based on wanting things we imagine as needs.

Jane Jacobs, who loves both cities and humans, writes about how a city begins. People find a friendly location perhaps on a river or at the confluence of rivers, or a seaside, or a place with rich fertile fields, or with forests or mineral riches. They plant themselves here, among the gifts of the earth. The city begins with a gift from the earth.[vii]

Human society begins with a gift from the earth. It continues with gifts from earth, air, water, plants, animals, all living things. Breathe the air. Gather berries, or grow a carrot. Engage with gifts.

In a gift-giving society, it would be obvious that one offers a gift in return —not payment, not creating a right to the thing received, but in appreciation and acknowledgment, as part of the relationship. Offering, giving and receiving, is the way of living communities. It is true for human communities, and is true for relationships among species and even those tight units of energy that we imagine are not conscious. We speak them into existence. Make an offering.

Remembering gift-giving, reclaiming gift-giving, like the Japanese bowl that is more beautiful after being mended, where the mending itself gives the beauty—what if we mend the brokenness of our exchanges, move away from the coldness of exchange, put some energy into creating the fabric of relationship? What if we live that way?

People find ways to give, of course, because giving makes us human, because we are only real in relationship. The best of relationships, even market relationships, include something human, a generosity of spirit, perhaps, ethics and honesty, giving your best work rather than the minimum.

TWELVE

HOW IT WORKS

Let's begin with a few remarks from indigenous people about how things really work. Their views are not filtered by a need to match modern science, support profit or growth, or maintain human superiority. That doesn't make them perfect, but it opens some possibilities.

The Kogi

The Kogi (pronounced Kogie) had hidden from outside society since about 1525, the time of the Spanish invasion of Colombia. In 1991 they sent a message through BBC journalist Alain Ereira, teaching us, "younger brother," to stop hurting the earth.[i] In 2012 they again contacted Ereira to make a second film, *Aluna*, the title referring to the spiritual force from which all things take their being. Their description of how the draining of lagoons and the blocking of estuaries harm the mountain exactly matches the observations of ecologists and biologists on the same topic.[ii]

Shall we wait until science catches up with the Kogi, or might we consider listening to the rest of what they say? We can just be a little more open to possibility if were willing to de-technologize the way we think about the workings of the world.

I like Charles Eisenstein's summary of some bits from *Aluna*:

SHODO SPRING

A black line, a network of hidden connections, links all the sacred places on earth. If that line should be broken, calamities will ensue, and this beautiful world shall perish. Destroying a forest here, draining a swamp there might have dire consequences across the globe. The Kogi shamans cannot perform their work of maintaining the balance of nature much longer in the face of our depredations.[iii]

For the Kogi, matter is not a container for thought; matter is thought made manifest, the thought of the Mother. Their beliefs are not actually supernatural, not in the sense of abstracting spirit (and all that goes with it like sacredness, consciousness, etc.) out from matter. To do so denies the inherent beingness of nature just as much as standard scientific materialism does.

Science is gradually catching up with them. Trees and forests and soils and mycelial networks are now understood to be vast communities that support each other, communicate, ask help and give it, warn of dangers, and learn.

The Kogi tell us, "You mutilate the world because you don't remember the Great Mother. If you don't stop, the world will die," and, "Do you think we say these words for the sake of talking? We are speaking the truth."

Nature is alive and intelligent. As our knowledge and technology fail us, we can open to other understandings.

Oaxaca

A group of Oaxacans wrote a comprehensive and historical statement and published it in *Permaculture Design Magazine*. The authors require that it be published in whole, with credits, or not at all. Here it is.

1. Much of the biodiversity that is found in our indigenous territories (around the world) is not merely the result of natural biological evolution, but rather is the product of and the

OPEN REALITY

accomplishment of thousands of years of scientific and communal investigation. Corn itself and many of the varieties of corn so coveted by northern corporations, for example, are creations of this communal science, which has been practiced for almost ten thousand years in Mesoamerica. When western investigators and academics come across this kind of biodiversity, they are not discovering anything "new," but rather the inventions, accomplishments and communal "property" of ancestral pueblos.

2. The reasons why this biodiversity still exists in these territories is important. It has been preserved by a civilization that does not value individualism, nor individual accumulation and privatization of property. When you enter into these indigenous territories, you are entering into another civilization... and into a different economic system where your intellectual property interests, interests in privatization and rights of ownership don't apply. YOU CANNOT PATENT COMMUNAL PROPERTY!!

3. The third reason is obvious to us, the indigenous peoples, but might pass unnoticed to you. Your Western civilization is in the process of reducing all of reality to its commercial value and placing a price on it. This concept is putting at risk your own civilization, economically, ecologically, and socially. For us, on the other hand, all beings, all things, and territories of this creation are sacred and deserve respect. This respect is the other reason why so much biodiversity still exists on our lands. The lack of respect for the sacredness of the planet is what is carrying Western civilization to self-destruction."[iv] [v]

These speakers use modern political language, and match what the Kogi said: Western civilization reduces reality to its commercial value, and that causes destruction. Privatization and individual accumulation do not work. Of course, the Oaxacan ancestors have been living interactively with the lands, forests, jungles, and animals for centuries, making small changes that help humans to live well, rather than completely sacrificing other beings for our behalf.

I add an observers comment from Derrick Jensen.

That movement toward depriving others of their subjectivity is the central movement of our culture. Indian after Indian has told me that the most basic difference between Western and Indigenous ways of being is that Westerners view the world as dead, not filled with speaking, thinking, feeling subjects as worthy and valuable as themselves.[vi]

If we start to listen, we might learn how to live.

The Commons

There's a sad story about how the commons work. Garrett Harding published this in 1968, following an earlier discussion of British economist William Forster Lloyd (1833). He called it "The Tragedy of the Commons." Basically it says that if everyone shares the same space (for grazing animals, for instance), then those who bring more animals will benefit and push out everyone else. The commons will be overgrazed and ruined for everyone.

The Tragedy of the Commons has been taught in economics schools for decades now. But it actually describes a very specific kind of situation: There is a limited space, that is not protected from outside intrusion. The people involved (in farming or grazing the commons) do not cooperate or speak to each other; there are no consequences for abuse. But it's taken to mean that communal ownership never works.

Elinor Ostrom researched successful and unsuccessful commons situations, and reported on what is needed for a lasting and productive commons. In summary, these are the rules for success:[vii]

1. Boundaries are clearly defined, for both the shared resource and group membership.
2. Members are rewarded fairly for their contributions.
3. Group members create at least some of their own rules and make their own decisions by consensus.
4. Monitoring: Group members can easily detect violations such as free-riding and active exploitation.
5. Sanctions are graduated, with stronger consequences after milder sanctions have been ignored.

OPEN REALITY

6. Conflict resolution mechanisms are perceived as fair by group members.
7. Groups have the authority to conduct their own affairs, not be governed from outside.
8. For groups that are part of larger social systems, there must be appropriate coordination among relevant groups.

The point is that people can work together, and often do, and the commons can thrive.

There was a bit of research news in September 2022, about the relationship between wildfires and grazing animals. It went like this: In areas where animals were grazing in the forests, wildfires were less. Grazing animals fight wildfires, thus they reduce climate change. Other articles cite the use of targeted grazing to discourage wildfires or speed recovery from fires.[viii]

There had already been a discussion of how much methane animal agriculture produced. Of course, most animal agriculture these days involves chickens in tiny cages eating grain instead of foraging in the woods, cattle on feedlots eating corn instead of roaming around and grazing, hogs in pens eating grain or sometimes dead animals instead of shrubs, or cattle clustered near a water source and grazing down to the roots.

When living naturally, animals eat better and produce less methane. They'll definitely trample the soil and fertilize it, they'll be healthier, and the result of that trampling will be healthy pastures that hold the rains instead of letting them slide down the hill in an erosion misery. This is how animals restore soils and reduce climate change.

Now we know that also prevents wildfires.

Those beautiful statements about being one with nature, respecting animals, seeing plants as relatives—they mean to actually stop making war on any of them. How do we learn to be members and participants in a plant/animal/insect system of life around us? Lean into this question. People are finding ways, and remembering them.

SHODO SPRING

This reminds me of Martín Prechtel's instructions:

There Has to Be Wild Land, Air, and Sea

> *There has to be more wild land that is unmined, unhiked, unrafted, unphotographed, unclimbed, unlogged, and uninhabited than there is land under cultivation, filled with habitation, dedicated to recreation, or otherwise put to use by humans. Together, wild plants, wild animals, wild people, unexplored places, unclimbed mountains, and headwaters, unrafted wild water, wild air, and the wild unanalyzed depths of anything are a giant culture comprised of a compendium of complex microcultures whose irrevocable right of ongoing presence and natural vitality is in direct proportion to the health of all people's domesticated unwild food, both plant and animal, and the health and wholeness of the people themselves.*[ix]

We have a similar thought from Nature Needs Half, an international coalition of scientists,[x] and from E.O. Wilson's Half Earth Project.[xi] Notice that "wild people" are included in wild lands.

Meanwhile, there are local and personal actions to take, more for the purpose of changing your own mind and habits than because they have a huge impact. Buy locally, buy handmade, make things, give things away. Start to recognize the difference between want and need. Luxuries gradually become necessities; keep them as luxuries. A hot bath, for instance, or a chocolate bar: luxuries.

Yet some necessities have turned to luxuries and need to return: trees, for instance, and the ability to walk under them and look up at the light and shadows in the leaves. Dirt that's safe to put your hands in, and time to do that. Child play, with other children or with bugs and snakes. Adult play, with children or adults or the moon. Eye contact, sunlight, moonlight, rolling down a hillside in snow or in summer's grass, burying each other in a pile of leaves or in a mound of sand at a beach. Water. A pickup ball game in a dead-end city street. A vacant lot and friends to turn it into a playground (a real one, with dirt and stones, sticks, gravel, dandelions and grass, with forts built from pallets, maybe a few scrubby trees and bushes, raspberries or mulberries—not

OPEN REALITY

an engineered one paved and plasticked and sterilized, then planted with so-called playground equipment because there's nothing to do there).

Where can we go from here? We can't return to gathering and hunting. There are too many of us for the land, even if it had not been terribly devitalized and degraded. And it has been ruined: fewer animals, fewer species, less nutrition in the ones that remain. Finally, we have not a clue about how to live that way. A few are trying to learn.

We have to find our own way. It's impossible to go back, and the way forward is not clear. It requires creativity. Openness. Listening.

THIRTEEN
BEYOND FALSE HOPE

The greatest challenge the Anthropocene poses isn't how the Department of Defense should plan for resource wars, whether we should put up sea walls to protect Manhattan, or when we should abandon Miami. It won't be addressed by buying a Prius, turning off the air conditioning, or signing a treaty. The greatest challenge we face is a philosophical one: understanding that this civilization is already dead. The sooner we confront our situation and realize that there is nothing we can do to save ourselves, the sooner we can get down to the difficult task of adapting, with mortal humility, to our new reality.[i]

—Bayo Akomolafe

He didn't say all humans will die. He said this civilization is already dead. I say, that means trying to save it is a waste of time. The noble plans for creating a real democracy, programs for renewable energy, Medicare for all, even regenerative agriculture are bandaids on cancer until something deeper is changed.

The question is, what will we do next? What kind of a civilization will replace this one? And what will we do to make it be more human?

SHODO SPRING

Talk with the land. Listen to the response. Allow yourself to fall in love with those beings we don't know or understand. Sure, fall in love with babies and humans of every kind too, but not only humans. The solution lies in the voices of the sagebrush, the wren, the river, the bur oak, and in our ability to hear them. The opening manifests in art, music, dance, and festival.

There are noble and beautiful people working to save civilization, or to transform it. I am thankful for them every day, for the gentling of people's daily lives and the truths being told.

Everything depends on the stories we tell ourselves.

"Hope is a longing for a future condition over which we have no agency," offers Derrick Jensen. That means we wait for someone else to solve our problems. I will name that false hope, because here is something else.

"Hope is uncertainty," says Rebecca Solnit. It's possibility, the opposite of despair. Hope is an opening into the future that allows for action. It's not a guarantee. We never know the outcome of our actions. Because of that, we are alive: not cogs in a machine on a predetermined path, but living conscious beings engaged with other living conscious beings, moving toward a future which is not in our control but just might be subject to our influence. We act on hope which is a possibility, we act again and again, widening the space in which life becomes possible. And remains possible.

Solnit tells this story from a speaking tour, from a group discussion:

> A small, elegant Asian woman about my age said, in a voice of bell-like clarity, "I think that is right. If I had not hoped, I would not have struggled. And if I had not struggled, I would not have survived Pol Pot."[ii]

Hope is essential. False hope is deadly, as is despair.

I don't think people choose despair. They are pushed into it, rather. They are advertised into it, terrorized into it, brutalized into it. Creating despair is a known method of psychological warfare.

OPEN REALITY

With climate change, hope could be the possibility that civilization survives, or that humans survive, even that ten humans survive, or that some form of life survives. Hope could be the simple possibility of human kindness, of learning how to live with each other again or for the first time, regardless of survival.

To nourish this hope, we sometimes tell stories of how people in the past or present have been kind to each other, to strangers, to animals, to plants, to mountains, to ecosystems. How people have risked their lives to defend the rice beds of northern Minnesota, or the sage grouse at Thacker Pass, or the water on which life depends, or a person or animal or anything.

Stories of Gaza and stories of the Warsaw Ghetto stand side by side here: A small thread of hope enables deeds of great courage. Even the self-immolation of Aaron Bushnell (February 27, 2024, over Gaza) carries the hope that someone will listen, that the sacrifice will change something.

We choose our stories. Please, choose with intention and awareness.

INTERLUDE: WHEN EVERYTHING IS CONSCIOUS

When the world, including concrete things, is understood as conscious, everything changes. The natural world (including animals, humans, and all the rest) is no longer a resource for our use. It exists in its own right and is worthy of respect. We as humans are nourished by it, including humans living today. As a philosophy, this is named *panpsychism.*[i]

Every speck of matter carries the quality of mind, awareness, consciousness. It's not necessarily personality or personal existence, more likely something we can't understand. There is nothing that is not conscious, down to the smallest particle, the electron, and up to interstellar space. We are embedded.

PART 3

HOW SHALL WE LIVE IN THESE TIMES?

Legend has it that one day there was a huge fire in the forest. All the animals fled in terror, for it was a terrible fire.

Suddenly the jaguar saw the hummingbird pass over her head in the opposite direction, going toward the fire. Soon she saw it happen again, this time in the same direction. She could observe this coming and going repeatedly, until she decided to ask the little bird, as it seemed a very odd behavior:

"What are you doing, hummingbird?" she asked.

"I go to the lake," and the bird took water with its beak and carried it to the fire to put out the fire.

The jaguar smiled. "Are you crazy? Do you think you're going to put out the fire with your little beak by yourself?"

"No," the hummingbird replied, "I know I can't. But that forest is my home. It feeds me, shelters me and my family, and I am grateful for that. And I help her grow by pollinating the flowers. I

SHODO SPRING

am part of her and she is part of me. I know I can't stop the fire, but I have to do my part."

At that moment the spirits of the forest that listened to the hummingbird, were moved by the little bird and its devotion to the forest. And miraculously they sent a strong downpour, which ended the fire.[i]

In these times, like times of huge conflagrations, how shall we live?

In a stable society not based on trauma, we imagine it would be easy, though none of us has experienced such a life. In a time of one crisis after another, we might pretend stability, but the results just don't work.

So how shall I live? How can I live with integrity and grace, being of benefit to the world around me rather than being part of the problem? How shall we live, those of us who recognize something is wrong and dangerous? And how do we find each other?

FOURTEEN
NECESSITY

Even when we understand that gatherers and nomads lived well for millennia, we can't go back. There are too many of us, and we've seriously depleted the living systems that once sustained a few millions of our ancient ancestors. Wild animals are replaced by domesticated, forests and prairies by monocrop agriculture, living soils by fertilized and poisoned dirt, and grasslands increasingly replaced by desert. Oceans are becoming lifeless, coral reefs dying, while once-sterile waters such as Lake Superior are newly full of living beings.

This points to two equal necessities.

Reduce Population and Consumption

I place these together because they are together. The environmental effect of a desert-living nomad, for instance, is vastly less than the impact of a king, a president, a captain of industry. This is obvious.

It is also obviously unthinkable for a few to be rich while others labor and starve. It's unnatural on the simple human level: We are designed as social creatures and this is fundamentally anti-social. It's also unsustainable on a practical level for myriads of reasons including rebellion and resistance in all its forms, and also the way arrogance and privilege interfere with good decision-making. (If the latter does not seem obvious to you, consider the quality of decisions made by whichever political party you dislike.) The wishes of the wealthy and powerful can no longer be taken as necessities. The needs of ordinary humans and all living beings are the actual necessities for our lives to continue.

Population matters. In 2024, July 25 was Earth Overshoot Day.[i] That's the date when humanity has used all the biological resources that Earth regenerates during the entire year, and starts living on stored resources.

In 1971, Earth Overshoot Day was in late December. Then, we were using just a little more than Earth produced. World population has more than doubled since then: from under four billion to nearly eight billion in 2020.[ii] Income inequality has increased tenfold,[iii] the income and wealth of the wealthiest have exploded,[iv] and their contribution to climate change is extreme.[v] We have to change all three: population, consumption, and inequality. (I encourage you to watch the excellent 20-minute lecture by Dr. William Rees, tagged at this endnote, for details and evidence.)[vi]

Restore the Fertility of the Earth

This grand instruction includes both sides of the equation: Stop destroying living things, and get serious about renewing them.

Here and there, this is being done. The ways that succeed do not involve high technology or expensive machines, but a completely different way of thinking. Holistic Management names this most clearly: It's a systems approach, learning how to think holistically first, then creating a detailed response for each individual situation. Permaculture and Regenerative Agriculture each have principles addressing the need to think holistically and to learn from the natural world.[vii] I'm remembering Regi Haslett-Marroquin explaining how he watches the chickens and then builds the fence just outside of their natural range.[viii]

More could be done if government funding supported these projects instead of propping up the fatally flawed industrial agriculture with death-dealing chemicals and monocultures.

Regenerating the earth is possible with existing knowledge, including

OPEN REALITY

traditional ways and modern ways. It requires a shift of resources from "growing the economy" to long-term survival and even well-being.

The Talmud states, "Do not be daunted by the enormity of the world's grief. Do justly now, love mercy now, walk humbly now. You are not obligated to complete the work, but neither are you free to abandon it."

FIFTEEN

NOBODY BUT US

There is no one but us. There is no one to send, nor a clean hand nor a pure heart on the face of the earth, nor in the earth, but only us, a generation comforting ourselves with the notion that we have come at an awkward time, that our innocent fathers are all dead as if innocence had ever been and our children unfit, not yet ready, having each of us chosen wrongly, made a false start, failed, yielded to impulse and the tangled comfort of pleasures and grown exhausted, unable to seek the thread, weak, and involved. But there is no one but us. There never has been.[i]

—Annie Dillard

We cannot wait for the technologists to fix it. The politicians won't do it; they are owned by the capitalists, who would rather go to Mars than heal this beautiful planet. Even you and I, well—I still have a car and a cell phone, and I write to you on this computer. Without fossil fuels I would be powerless, or so it seems, unable to talk with others, to go and protest, or to buy my groceries or visit my grandchildren.

But there is no excuse for not acting in whatever positive ways we can. Once we know, we are required to respond.

In 2023, 24, 25, we know. Wildfires, floods and droughts surround us. As Albert Einstein said, "The problems we are facing cannot be solved with the level of thinking that created them."

Here's a to-do list, much like a list one might make for a personal health crisis: Admit there's a problem. Do basic self-care. Get professional help. Ask for spiritual help and healing. Stay responsible. Tell ourselves the truth.

My own world is on fire, almost literally. Looking at a world map of present wildfires is horrifying. Maps of droughts are equally frightening. Since 2021, when the Boundary Waters, Minnesota's iconic wilderness, closed for firefighting—fire started from lightning, not careless camping when the smoke drifted down to southern Minnesota—every year from now on will be warmer, drier, wetter, with more fires, floods, droughts, and hunger. Until we stop it and turn it around. All the state and national governments I know are still supporting disastrous profit-driven policies.

Admit that climate change is happening. Also the political world is near flames, and the health of the natural world is shaky in many ways beyond climate change. Theres a problem. We've now labeled it a polycrisis.

Basic self-care. Stop it from getting worse. And stay out of fights: I avoid conspiracy discussions as much as I humanly can. More, I avoid seeing people as monsters, even those who are clearly doing damage. In conversations that are polarizing, I slow down, attempt to be a calm voice, or just don't participate. More and more, I'm backing away from ridicule of even the worst people.

> Rumi: "Beyond ideas of wrongdoing and rightdoing there's a field. Ill meet you there."

About climate change, I practice living as if industrial civilization is already broken, and also practice gratitude for amazing impermanent things like cars, central heating, internet, everything that makes my first-world life so easy and that must be abolished if the human species is to survive.

OPEN REALITY

Stop it from getting worse. To withdraw from the insane web of consumerism is both a very small act and a deep personal change. To create a lively web of mutual support and exchange is a radical and powerful action. The corporate ways are in trouble; you can tell by the ever-increasing violence required to keep them in place.[ii] When humane, earth-based communities are strong and stable enough, the rigid and violent structures will show themselves as a hollow shell and crumble easily. Well, relatively easily. It will still be hard to live without cars, airplanes, and the whole structure of industry.

I quoted Annie Dillard because her words so strongly say that we must do it and not wait for someone else. Yet it is not quite true that we are alone. Rather, we are surrounded. The world is full of creators, rich in allies. When we open up, they appear. But we cannot lie around waiting for them. At the least, we must first stop fighting against them, stop interfering with their movement, stop treating them as objects and resources for our convenience.

Three Paths, the Great Turning, What We Are Doing

Joanna Macy looks at our situation and describes three paths in The Great Turning. One is "holding actions," just stopping the harm. Putting your body in the path of a pipeline, blowing the whistle on the harmful doings of government or industry or whoever needs to be stopped, general strikes and mass gatherings—this is what we usually call activism or resistance. The second is building the new world, creating structures that grow food, care for humans, relate to the natural world, everything in a way that is more humane and open, supporting life instead of death. The third is consciousness change.

Today's leading activist groups do two or three of these at once. At the Unist'ot'en Camp in British Columbia, indigenous ways are practiced, with buildings placed in the path of the pipeline; ceremony and traditional hunting/gathering/smoking/drying happen together with blockading logging trucks and confronting agents of abuse from industry and government alike. While court battles and treaty negotiations continue. Blocking harm on every level; creating the new society; offering a different consciousness by practicing it. "It's not about rights, it's about our responsibility to the land, and teaching nonnative guests how to abandon our habitual arrogance and live in harmony." —Mel Bazil, Gitxsan Nation, 2012.

At Standing Rock in 2016, an amazing community grew up to take care of people, in context of morning prayers and songs, feeding and health care and latrines and building and child care and giving shelter, while some went to the front lines to meet the police, to say no directly. Some say they lost that battle; the Dakota Access Pipeline runs dangerous oil by the tribal lands and across the river and above the aquifer but the battle of spirit went another way. "*Mni Wiconi*," "Water is Life," are the spirit words, "water protector" our name for each other, and the new tradition is to follow indigenous leaders. Recognizing the bankruptcy of mainstream, industrialized, capitalist settler culture, a small beginning step is to join a culture which, though not whole because it has been bombarded and assaulted for centuries, still holds a sense of how to participate in the world.

In 2021 at Red Lake Treaty Camp in Minnesota, it was the same: traditional community, solidarity, and absolute resistance to the destruction being wrought by drilling equipment and pipeline building. Risking lives for protection. Raising understanding of what it means to be Treaty People—and we all are treaty people, even if our ancestors arrived on this land decades after the last treaty. Treaties bind us together, define our boundaries, create a language of what matters and how we can possibly live together with our differences.

Thacker Pass, Peehee Mu'huh, Nevada, began January 15, 2020, as a holding action, focused directly on consciousness change. Yes, there are beautiful and endangered animals and plants that would be damaged by the f-thousand-acre lithium mine, as would sacred sites of the Northern Paiute and Western Shoshone people. But the point is to confront the illusion of alternative energy—that we can eat our cake and have it, that we can continue industrial civilization by switching to solar and wind energy, electric vehicles, and so forth—all of which depend on lithium batteries for energy storage.

The resisters at Thacker Pass are not pointing out that it can't be done because eventually we will have mined all the lithium. They are not suggesting developing hemp batteries or some alternative. They are

OPEN REALITY

simply pointing straight at the fundamental flaw in this society: that we are willing to sacrifice anything for our own convenience. Our definition of progress is to convert the living earth into money, forests into pavement, and so forth. Two white guys, Max Wilbert and Will Falk, both committed activists, pitched a tent there in the winter, and as spring moves forward the local tribes are holding events, nearby ranchers are raising their voices, and the message about industrial civilization is making its way into mainstream media, while supporters come to the camp.

2024 update: The bulldozers are moving, the tribes and organizers are making a stand in court, and around the world communities are objecting to lithium mining. A quick internet search showed protests in Argentina, Chile, Serbia (successful), Tibet (temporarily successful), Portugal, and in the United States: Nevada, Oregon, North Carolina, and the Black Hills.[iii] In African nations such as Zimbabwe, Namibia, and Democratic Republic of Congo, controversy and legal battles are more common than on-the-ground protests.[iv]

Each of these is a holding action, AND a call to remember our spiritual relationships, AND a creation of the kind of community that might make wiser decisions about how to live on and with the earth. Resistance communities live in a special place, and there's no certainty that they'll stay pure and noble when power shifts. They are a beginning that must be made, a ground for learning how to live together.

Nonviolence

Theres such a vast discussion about appropriate and effective methods, that I hesitate to even address this. Whatever I say, there will be vigorous controversy. I'll just make a few notes.

First, nonviolence is frequently confused with pacifism, even in dictionaries. Pacifism is a moral commitment to a path of not harming others in order to maintain ones personal integrity regardless of the results. Gene Sharp, formerly a pacifist, became the primary spokesperson for strategic nonviolence: using non-harming methods because they are more effective in the long run, and safer in the short term. Sharp has written extensively, and much of his work is available online.[v] Martin Luther King, Jr. also writes eloquently on the vital distinction between nonviolence and pacifism in his book *Stride Toward Freedom*.

In the early 2000s, Erica Chenoweth extensively researched the question of effective action. She had made a bet with someone about that question; her original position was that violence would be more effective. The research changed her mind:[vi] When about 3.5% of a population engage in sustained and active resistance, they win. (It's easier to attract larger numbers of people with nonviolence, because the risks are lower and the morality is clearer.) As people from all parts of society start to participate, those who work in government or corporate sectors start to re-evaluate their allegiance. That includes police, who are supposed to enforce the status quo but might not. It helps to have leaders, to be able to change tactics quickly, to have clear communication channels (including consensus processes).

Community Rights Organizing

This very particular kind of nonviolent action works in places like the United States that claim to be democratic but are actually in thrall to giant corporations or outside forces. It's generally done in response to a crisis.

When a local community is threatened by something they don't want, such as a giant hog farm, waste disposal plant, mine, fossil fuel pipeline, or the like, theres a process.

OPEN REALITY

Locals talk with each other and come to agreement that they don't want it. (Catch: a lot of local people will be eager for even temporary jobs because they want to feed their kids or send them to college. Often they don't notice the other livelihoods being ruined by the new "job-producer," such as farming, fishing guides, tourism, wild rice harvests, forest products.)

1. If a group of people agree, they can start with the basic definition of government in their country. In the U.S. its officially based on the consent of the governed. Powers are reserved to the people unless specifically designated otherwise, and so forth. They begin to enforce that definition.

2. They pass local ordinances asserting their rights to protect themselves, to enjoy clean water and natural beauty and quality of life. Sometimes they also name rights of rivers and natural communities "to exist, flourish, and naturally evolve." Sometimes the ordinance includes methods to defend these rights.

3. The State sues them and fines them. The corporation threatens them.

4. Sometimes they win. Sometimes they give up after a series of losses. State governments are usually deeply intertwined with coal, agribusiness, fossil fuels, and other toxic industries, (another catch, accepted as normal but properly defined as corruption).

5. And sometimes, after doing everything right and still losing, people are radicalized.[vii] Having become closer to their neighbors than ever before, they have a newly clear view of the structures that harm our lives and communities.

In conversation with long-time Community Rights organizer Paul Cienfuegos, after two of us expressed hopelessness about ever being able to work with right-wingers, Paul told us he had led dozens of workshops across the country, year after year, with politically diverse groups, in which the participants were able to focus together to stop corporate harms threatening their local communities, and were consistently able to ignore issues that would normally have divided them. He also said that once they got to know each other, because of mutual trust they were able to tiptoe into the difficult issues. After he said that, I remembered my year in community organizing, when we worked with racism simply by having people sitting in the same room working on issues together.[viii]

"Protect your spirit, because you are in the place where spirits get eaten."

—*John Trudell*

SIXTEEN

FINDING THE WILL

Without a vision of what life could be, how can we find the will to move forward?

Imagine a way of living that is whole. We know bits and pieces; almost no one knows the whole, even fragments from memory. So imagine. Give yourself a few months, a summer or a winter, to allow your mind to shift. I encourage you to do this together with others, because it is together that we make change.

Gather in circle with a few people even just one, not more than ten and say to each other how a whole life seems to you. What might a day be like, in that dream? A week? Speak and listen to all the dreams, let them blend together. Do this many times, with the same people, with different people. Do it again, until you know each other and your shared intention. If you gather weekly, you can create a tapestry from all your imaginings. (A weekend or a whole day would also work.)

Search your memory for those bits and pieces that have already happened in your life, and speak them to each other. The great-aunt who listened to your troubles; exploring the creek with your sister; going to the corner store with your best friend. Having a best friend, doing everything together. Giving a dinner party, messing it up, and being rescued by the mother-in-law you didn't even like. Being caught

67

in a hailstorm and suddenly finding shelter. Getting a ride from a stranger when you were stranded. Speak together of the places in your own lives where community already lived, where life was whole even briefly.

Remember times when you have felt safe. Notice whether your first memory is about physical safety, emotional, social, self-esteem, or something else, and notice the body sensations that go with feeling safe. Relaxed belly? Shoulders drop? If asking the question brings up memories of feeling unsafe, notice these as well. What makes the internal experience of safety? It includes physical sensations and thoughts.

Practices: Intentionally generate the body awareness that you associate with a memory of safety. Do it more than once, until it becomes familiar; carry that feeling into your next situation (difficult or easy).[i] Another practice is to find a place, posture, and orientation where your body feels best.[ii] This too can be remembered and carried into hard situations. The impossible becomes possible, or the unbearable bearable. (To write instructions would be another book. You can find instructions or guided meditations in many places. Let me recommend Kristin Neff and Tara Brach, for starters, and qigong exercises about fear, from YouTube or elsewhere.)

These details, one moment at a time, become a foundation for building the dream life together. You can't do it alone. Daring to speak them aloud, even only to the one who is your safest person in the world, begins to make the imagining real. This is a treasure; cherish it and share it.

On your own now, spend a day noticing what in your life feels like wholeness. This is a body awareness. It might mean noticing a subtle relaxation, or a warmth, an energy, a calming, a lightness. Or just happiness. Some thoughts happen with it. Try to catch the sensation first, and then the thoughts. Is this rare, or does it happen often for you? How do the next minutes change after such a moment? Can you invite it? Or do you need help to even begin?

Again, **speak of these to at least one other person**, a group if possible. If you're part of a family or an intimate group, you could start a custom of sharing such things.

OPEN REALITY

What we acknowledge becomes more real, and still more when we share it. With our bodies and our voices and our listening, we are changing the structure of reality.

We've been living in a structure that is cold, punitive, unfair; mistakes get punished, greed rewarded, truth-telling too often ridiculed or imprisoned. This is made by humans. It can be changed. I wrote about its making in Chapters 6 through 11. We need to make a way of being that is warm, friendly, human, connected, to make a space that is safe for all. We do it in small acts, conscious acts.

Of course, this isn't all of it. There is also "Practice random acts of kindness and senseless beauty." There is definitely "Pay it forward." There is addressing injustice and taking bold stands to protect water, earth, humans, animals, all of life. Community naturally grows in the process of such actions.

When we think about creating alternatives to the colonizing, exploitive way of life, we need a place to stand. This little exercise could be a beginning of finding that place. Or it could be a renewal ritual, whether daily, weekly, yearly, at the new moon, or on your own schedule.

Recognizing Community

What good is this awareness, for our intention of living in wholeness?

I'm in debt to so many people, I can't possibly name them all. Wil came to help me install the front door. Justin replaced the basement door and wouldn't take money. Linne spent a day taking me to major dental surgery and three more days making sure I had what I needed for recovery. Perry organized a group of volunteers and a wood splitter, and that winter I heated the house with firewood instead of propane.

Gather again. Speak to each other of those moments, the ones this week, or even just today. Acknowledge what is already here. Remind each other of what you have known. Speak to each other of the moments of wholeness in your life with people, with other humans. Do this before you talk about experiences of intimacy with animals or plants. Create the human container first, if you can. If you are very hurt by other humans, begin wherever is easiest, and it's fine if it's the tree at the corner or the forsythia bushes by the creek.

SHODO SPRING

These Are Seeds for What We Can Grow

Some of us had parents who experienced deep nourishment, who were able to pass it on to us—nourishment of community, plants and animals, joyful work, courageous action, creativity, spirituality. Others had parents who loved us unremittingly, even if they expressed it by "Put on your jacket" or "Don't talk back." Fewer grew up embedded in a lively community, every adult an aunt or uncle, ceremonies and traditions part of everyday life, even if cousin Sue had been kidnapped or brother Joe was in jail. We can draw on whatever bits and pieces of community we have known. Life supports us.

We need to imagine wholeness. All the better if we can remember it, if our bodies know it. And then we share it.

The lasting source-fire comes from the life dream and from love. Those of us who build alternative communities are doing real work, bringing the dream into real life in detail. People who volunteer to take meals to elders and the homebound, who make human connections, are doing real work, making community. So much real work, good work is being done all around us.

I watch it happening. In the middle of destruction, even in the middle of climate change, we see the restoration of lands through regenerative agriculture, cultural fire management, planting by listening. Indigenous nations are reclaiming culture and protecting their people in very tangible ways, along with sacred runs and walks and rides, ceremonies and gatherings. And the resistance to industrial destruction includes thousands of people based in groups following indigenous leadership.

SEVENTEEN
VALUES

Identifying your values is a way of knowing who you are, making you stronger and more able to do the things that need to be done. Talking about values with friends and family brings you closer together, and more effective even if some values differ. Speaking of values across political or religious differences has a healing potential beyond knowing.

You could use these in journal work, in a discussion group, or perhaps in artistic work in poem, song, visual art, creative protest. (Notice how values appear in the work of others.)

Five Questions

I offer you f questions, heard from Derrick Jensen on YouTube[i] with added comments of my own.

- **What do you love?** What or whom do you love so much that you would give everything, even give your life, for their well-being?
- **What are your gifts?**

SHODO SPRING

- **What is the largest thing you can accomplish with those gifts that are unique to you in the whole universe?**
- **What does your land base need to survive?** This seems out of sequence, yet it's a key part of the whole. Land base means that land area that supports our life. If the land base dies, so do we.
- **Are you going to do it?** Having imagined a life work, will you stretch and embrace it, let it create you, let it give you life as you push beyond your own imagination? Or will you go watch TV?

I add these questions for studying yourself:

- What makes you happy? What kind of activities, places, food, people, opportunities help you feel personally better, satisfy your needs, help you relax? And the opposite: What makes you unhappy?
- What are you afraid of losing? Or who (individuals or a kind of people) do you dislike, and why?
- What do you long for?
- What do you want people to say about you, about your character, about your accomplishments? True things, I mean. If you're being introduced for an award, what would you want them to say? Or write your epitaph, your obituary. Don't be shy; imagine you are at your best and have all the help in the world; what would it say?

Your answer to every one of these questions is a confession, which means an acknowledgment or avowal. Please confess to yourself your dreams, whether you long to be noble, to be famous, or to be comfortable, or to serve. Know who you are.

EIGHTEEN
MENDING INTO LIFE

There is a Japanese tradition, Kintsugi, when a bowl is broken, of mending it with gold so that it becomes more beautiful than before.

We can see this too in human beings, people who have come through immeasurable tragedy and have healed to become wisdom and peace for those around them.

It matters that the mending is of gold. A bowl mended only with glue is simply a mended bowl for everyday use, not brought out for guests or admired. Gold, of course, represents all that is best, pure, uncontaminated.[i] It's mixed with lacquer to make a bond that holds.

When people mend, what is the gold? Surely it involves love, care, respect. Understanding of how the wounds are made, and how to heal them. Or maybe not. Maybe simply the forces of nature, immersion in the mystery. I remember a woman who told of going to a cabin in the woods, staying there alone until the trees healed her. There is the long prayer, the going down into the tomb, the womb, the cave, the depths until something moves, until one rises up reborn, comes back from hades, broken and changed and healed. In my Zen tradition, we do it together, with long hours of silent meditation and more hours of silence.

SHODO SPRING

With what gold might we be mended to be more beautiful than before, to again hold water or tea or food for our people, for all peoples? What healing could bring us to our deepest and better selves, more whole than before?

I think that process has begun, even as we begin to recognize the failure of our culture. There is a cultural edge of people studying ourselves, asking the questions, doubting what we've been taught without jumping to conclusions about answers. Learning to listen and to follow, to open, to be willing to heal; making awkward guesses, being clumsy, being fools all belong to the first step on the path.

I wrote about mending with gold, and now I propose that we must become the gold that mends our own culture, mends its brokenness, mends the way it has shaped itself around centuries of trauma, even millennia of trauma.

There's a problem with this image of mending. The bowl to be mended is brittle, ceramic, inflexible. It is not a living thing, but created from something flexible that was baked to become hard. I think our culture is like this: burnt in the fire of militarism and capitalism, ruined, turned into what is not alive. A culture needs to be alive. If not, it breaks. And it hurts people, because there is no space for life.

If we are not creating a beautiful, rigid, fragile art object, what can mending mean?

We want a culture as full of life as a cubic inch of soil, as the ocean before pollution or perhaps the ocean resisting pollution. How do we become the ones who can do that?

Perhaps the bowl needs to be broken, no, pulverized, and returned to become part of the soil again.

Grass grows through the cracks in a sidewalk and eventually takes it over. Tree roots break any pavement. Living things undo dead things, even those made with a loving effort. Mice ate the fabric of a beautiful dress I had loved. The driveway, no matter how well built, eventually succumbs to brush and weeds.

My friend Martin Bulger in is an extraordinary healer. Recently he said, in a class on physical healing: "It's not about getting rid of something. It's

OPEN REALITY

about finding out who you are in that place [that painful place in your body]."

Here we are in a broken society, asking about healing. Who are you in that place?

Who are we in this place, the place of injustice and suffering?

There is a meditation described by Stephen Levine that might be helpful. In it, after settling down in your own body-mind, you imagine your self expanding to fill the room, the building, the town, the region, the continent, the earth, the solar system, the galaxy, the universe as far as you can imagine. Look back toward the earth, toward your self and your people. Feel small. If you have an enemy, notice their smallness too.

Stay as long as you like. Gradually let yourself become a little smaller, a little smaller, bringing the vastness down with you as you return to this body. Rest there a while.

If you like, repeat this exercise with one modification. After settling into your body, look in your heart for the goodness that is there. You can personify it as Jesus, Buddha, any being of purity and spaciousness, or simply a light, with whatever color and texture call to you. Allow that light, that image, to grow, to fill your physical body, and so forth out to the reaches of the universe, allowing the holy to fill all space and time. And then come back gradually to the body. Allow awareness of the enemy as this sacredness expands and contracts; if you notice changes in the field, simply notice, as you notice changes in your own field.

It might be a good thing to do this meditation with a group, especially with your spiritual group, your family, or friends. Or do it in a place that feels contentious; you can be very inconspicuous in a public space. I've done that quiet, personal ceremony in the context of a loud and angry demonstration. And then, you can do it in the safest and most sacred place you know.

Doing this changes the structure of space, in our own awareness and also holographically, to affect everything around us.

NINETEEN
LIVED BY ALL BEINGS

Everything lives us. Everything breathes us into life. Everything witnesses us into being. And we in turn live, breathe, and witness them into existence. In Buddhism this is called interdependent co-arising. Things arise and things fall, dependent on each other, linked together irrevocably. We are neither separate nor permanent, but completely embedded in the web of life, with a spark of awareness in this individual being, as in other individual beings. We look out at each other, and recognize each other. Our mutual seeing/hearing/smelling/tasting/sensing is how we create each other. This is not limited to humans.

There's an image in physics, of matter as concentrated energy, or a disruption in the space-time continuum. It's not flat, it curves. Space is like hills and valleys, sculpted by the substances we call matter.

My own image of matter is as concentrated consciousness. I think of both matter and energy as just shapes and movement in the mind-field. Space is alive. There's enormous energy in a cubic inch of intergalactic space. Everything around us is alive and conscious. Plants, fungi, mycelia, cells, bacteria. Rocks, minerals, waters. Atoms, molecules, quarks. The billions of tiny creatures that make up half our own body weight. I name them to invoke them, to invite them here as witnesses and co-creators. We are created by everything.

SHODO SPRING

This sense of everything as alive is called animism.[i] Most indigenous religions are animistic, and deeply based in their local geography. I've been pleased to find a tradition of Buddhist animism, and to discover how many other contemporary Buddhists are living it too.

Everything is alive, not in the sense of biological life, but as a mystery that doesn't fit into words. Every single thing is not a *thing* but an unknown, not solid but uncontrollable. I am calling that alive.

We live in a society deeply based on Buddhism's three poisons of greed, anger, and self-delusion, with the core poison being the illusion of separation. It's combined with an idea that other things are lifeless or unimportant and available for our use.

There's a story in David Abram's first book, *The Spell of the Sensuous*, in which he studies with shamans in Indonesia. The local people put out offerings for the little people. Curious, he goes to watch what happens with the offerings. He sees hundreds of ants, lining up and walking to the bowl of rice, and carrying off the rice one grain at a time until the bowl is empty. He tells his hosts, and they look at him oddly. Finally he understands that he had not understood.[ii]

They knew that "little people" meant ants. They did not think "little people" were some kind of magical creature, or had no bodies, or were anything but the visible little beings seen all the time.

If ants deserve offerings, then ants are magical beings in themselves. As are we, incidentally, and all the larger animals. Animals at least; no comment yet about plants, rocks, rivers, mountains but really, we already know about them.

When Dereck Fiddler, a Lakota holy man, gave me a rattle and told me it was associated with the little people, he told me how to make offerings: "They like Skittles, and they like soda pop." I objected to the soda, and he said fruit juice would be acceptable. I made an offering with Skittles and orange juice, and watched the ants come.

Daniel Quinn describes two ways of being: those who live as gods, and those who live in the hands of the gods. To live as gods involves control, or the illusion of control, and the right to do anything to the non-gods around you.

OPEN REALITY

In the hands of the gods, you are not guaranteed a long life, enough to eat, or immortality. But you are part of a community.

We don't need to know what will happen next. We want to know, so we can plan, control, feel secure. But there is no security. Everyone will die, whether sooner or later and by whatever means. There is nothing at all that we can rely on. That is a place we can stand.

Martín Prechtel says that a shaman mends the hole in the fabric of society. That image is worth everything.

Mending the holes. I said before, becoming the gold that mends. Now this: Society is not a bowl, but a fabric. It's soft, flexible, strong. It holds together, is composed of interwoven threads. To mend it, then, involves being soft, flexible, strong, connected. Bringing ourselves to connection with earth and with other humans and other conscious beings, we weave and re-weave. I've done mending, lots of it, and darning, a little. To weave through the hole, back and forth, carefully connecting new threads with the old, interweaving them thoroughly lest the whole thing fall apart as soon as it is worn and so the new weaving may be as flexible as the old—now we are doing something alive. And that alive something must be fully connected with the aliveness of the old society, the old fabric, the old sock or it will tear apart.

It is possible that Martín's healing only works in a village-scale society, where there is a flexible fabric. It's possible that our society's damage may be too severe. Still, what if we did a thousand tiny mendings, or a million? What if, every time we did an act of kindness, we dedicated it to the healing of the whole fabric of society? What if a billion of us did this?

Ancient Zen master Dizang said, "Not knowing is most intimate."

When I invite you to not-knowing, it's an invitation to act without expectations. Because the only thing we own is our own life, the actions we have already taken. Because our actions create our lives and the world we live in, and the world others live in too: We all create it together. Actions based on guarantees—"If I do this, that good thing will happen"—are marketplace transactions, and they are part of the problem. Please act from love, act with integrity, without worries about outcome. (Okay, worry if you like.) No promises except the reality of this moment.

I'd like to end with a quotation from David Abram, who says this in very poetic language:

> The animate earth around us is far lovelier than any heaven we can dream up. But if we wish to awaken to its richness, well need to give up our detached, spectator perspective, and the illusion of control that it gives us. That is a terrifying move for most over-civilized folks today—since to renounce control means noticing that we really are vulnerable: to loss, to disease, to death. Yet also steadily vulnerable to wonder, and unexpected joy.
>
> For all its mind-shattering beauty, this earth is hardly safe; it is filled with uncertainties, and shadows—with beings that can eat us, and ultimately will. I suppose thats why contemporary civilization seems so terrified to drop the pretense of the view from outside, the God trick, the odd belief that we can master and manage the earth.
>
> But we can't master it—never have, never will. What we can do is to participate more deeply, respectfully, and creatively in the manifold life of this breathing mystery were a part of.[iii]

TWENTY

CHANGING THE STRUCTURE OF REALITY

Meditation and ritual change the structure of reality.

The laws of nature, the laws of physics and biology, chemistry and genetics are still there. There is another level, the level of energy, thought, consciousness. Matter is embodied consciousness. Long ago, as a physics student, I got a sense of this. They said matter is concentrated energy. Now some people say information. I say now, matter is consciousness, which does not imply human-like consciousness.

Zen Master Dogen said in thirteenth-century Japan, "All beings are Buddha nature." He contradicted the best teaching of his time, that beings HAVE Buddha nature. He took it a step further. For the moment, let's not try to pin down "Buddha nature" into something permanent or solid. It has a feeling of life, consciousness, being awake. And it's not a possession, not even a quality of things or people. It's our essence.

Consciousness is who we are and what we are. This doesn't deny bones and muscles, or electrons and molecules, but includes them. Everything is mine, not "everything is imagination" but "everything is consciousness." I have started to use the term "panpsychism" which simply means everything is consciousness. Not just dogs, trees, and flowers. Not even just soil, rocks, and water. Everything is consciousness.

SHODO SPRING

This is why subtle energies work, why homeopathy works, why flower essences actually change things in peoples mind and emotion and intention. It's probably also why it's so hard to pin them down, why we can't usually measure such things.[i] It's also why placebos work.

Then there is mind and emotion—not sure which is first—then the physical level. The forces we call energy—electricity, gravity, magnetism—those are in the physical world.

Traditional peoples recognized those energies. They gave names to many of them, not just one. Because with every bit of matter there is also energy. And then there are the names for complex collections of matter: Gaia, for one, aka Mother Earth in many languages. Matter carries energy and matter is consciousness consolidated as the physicists said about matter being concentrated energy. $E=mc^2$.

Meditation Changes the Structure of the Universe

There are rules that say only the mundane exists and there is no sacred. Those are human rules and meditation changes them. The rules that say you are alone, or the rules that say you are supreme: It changes both of these, the miserable and the arrogant versions of isolation.

Meditation removes those rules. It creates an opening in which everything is open and flexible, things are allowed to be as they are. Things create each other. In meditation its possible to receive the creation of all the other beings of the universe, not just the devas but the rocks and waters too. It's possible to send out creation into them, to recognize the flow of mutual creation, sometimes called interdependence.

In ritual, I think, we offer a structure to the universe. We prepare ourselves through rituals of purification—ceremonial handwashing, or smudging, incensing our robes, making prostrations—and then we enter a space ritually created and named as sacred. We say the names that we have given to those great forces, and we honor them, offer energy to them in the form of chanting or actions. We express gratitude, the most powerful of all mental states. We express praise. We feed the spirits or beings or great forces, whatever we call them. We describe the nature of this relationship, through our chants or prayers or through sermons,

OPEN REALITY

dharma talks, or stories. And we ask for help. The relationship goes in all directions, so ritual includes both offering and asking.

And then we take our leave from the heightened awareness of this level of existence. In one way or another we return to the mundane, hopefully carrying some of that consciousness with us. Dainin Katagiri Roshi, my first Zen teacher, taught us that when we left the zendo we bow to the zendo that is out there, everywhere in the whole world. The whole world is the zendo; the whole world is the sacred place; the whole world is the place for spiritual practice.

Doing ritual indicates a specific structure, connected with a particular tradition and people. When I first came to Zen I resisted the structures, because I had embraced ways offered by some ancient European earth religions. I also had a resistance to anything that reminded me, even a little, of the church in which I grew up. Still, over years, the depth of the Zen style crept into my bones, and now it is my home.

Indigenous religions belong to a people and are rooted in the land. Islam is clear: Bow toward Mecca five times a day. The Dakota recognize the origin of the universe at Bdote, a place where I've been, in what we now call Minneapolis; the Lakota find home in the Black Hills, the Hopi at the *sipapu,* probably what we call the Grand Canyon. Every people belongs to a different place.

There are sacred places. Not all religions have them. Both Buddhism and Christianity honor places but in a different way. I will not be surprised to learn land-roots in these two religions that have been my home, but finding those roots will be someone else's work.

Sacred places matter. You can feel them when you go there. You can also bring forth the sacredness of a place, by acknowledging and offering, and coming back again and again, making offerings and doing ceremony. I am learning this at the land where I live: It matters to keep coming back to the places. The spirits hear you when you speak to them. Maybe, eventually, you begin to hear them. Sometimes, at the place here called the Central Altar, I think I see them in the bluff. They come and go. Sometimes, at the river, or at the North Altar, I feel them. Once, upstream on the creek, they gave me a song.

83

Zazen

I said meditation, but I meant zazen.

In Zen, we use the word "zazen" for what most people call "sitting meditation." The reason is that meditation is a very confusing word. Many people meditate in order to calm down. Some people do guided meditations or visualizations to manifest things, whether better health, prosperity, love, or even peace on earth. Zazen is not like that. We use a different word to make it really clear that were not talking about a goal-directed activity.

My teacher Shohaku Okumura told me once, "If you're sitting zazen to get enlightened, you're still doing business." His teachers teacher, Kodo Sawaki Roshi, famously said, "Zazen is good for nothing."

Thirty years ago, when I was a baby Zen student, Teijo Munnich gave a talk that changed my understanding forever. She had been looking at a text that referred to the monks "disporting themselves in zazen." She looked up "disport" and it means "play." She thought there must have been a translation error, and she looked up the Japanese characters translated as "disport." There were two characters, both of which meant "play." Here are some current definitions of the archaic word disport: "enjoy oneself unrestrainedly; frolic, to divert or amuse (oneself), to play in a carefree way or to amuse yourself in a lighthearted fashion." It comes from the French word *desporter*, which means "to carry away" or "to entertain." Think of *disport* as what kids do when they have so much fun playing that they get carried away, forgetting all about school until the bell rings.[ii]

Looking at a person sitting immobile on a cushion, likely in the company of others, its hard to imagine this is play or frolic. But we're invited to it.

Now consider the data on children needing play and how their brains and lives are affected when they live the civilized life with pavement, electronics, and control.[iii] Let me mention what play really means, drawing from O. Fred Donaldson's *Playing by Heart*.[iv]

Play is what you do with no goal. Play is a natural expression of the life force.

OPEN REALITY

I remember running across the dewy grass on an early summer morning, for the sheer pleasure of muscles engaging and the sweet air in my breath. I remember turning cartwheels on that grass, over and over again for hours, trying to master it—for the pleasure of my body on the earth and the experience of engaging muscles in action.

And I remember going every spring into the wild spaces, looking for the iris that I had found there just once, the most beautiful thing I had ever seen. There have been many such "most beautiful things" since, but that may have been the first time I had the thought. The delicate petals arching up and curving down, the shades of lavender, and the fragrance—two plants under the spruce trees, a few blossoms. The next year I searched for weeks, but they didn't bloom until May. I memorized the time as well as location so I could find them again, every year until we moved when I was twelve.

They've been paved over now. A development was built on my wild spirit-home. And other iris are blooming now outside my door.

The one wild place that nobody can take away from us is this body and mind. And it is wild. The human body contains more than ten thousand microbial species.[v] In their three percent of body weight are thousands of characters that are not us, that are untamed. To be healthy human animals, we need them to stay wild. In this space, efforts to control simply don't work.

I won't say anything about the mind being wild. If you think your mind is under control, you are probably spending a lot of energy keeping it that way and not even noticing.

Sitting zazen is about allowing things to be as they are. The mind produces thoughts. We normally take these thoughts as proof that we exist. (Descartes: "I think, therefore I am.") We want to exist, we want to be real, and we have a mistaken idea that its either existence or annihilation. So its hard to back away from the evidence that "I have these thoughts, therefore there is an 'I' who has these thoughts, therefore I'm real." Actually, thoughts just happen.

People think Buddhists see everything as illusion. It's an understandable mistake. The illusion is about permanence and absolute existence. We do exist—in change. We are created every moment, by things around us

SHODO SPRING

as well as by our past. We are real. To me, an apple tree is more "real" than a cement wall, so I'm using the word real in a biased way. (The cement wall is also changing, it's just hard for us to notice.) We are alive, we are life, we are change. And we are completely interconnected with everything.

Sitting zazen is about letting that be so, giving up the fight for control and for permanence. When we lose that fight, we can be alive. This is how zazen is play.

I'm reminded of the story of Jacob wrestling with God, and losing.[vi] He received a new name, Israel, meaning "he struggles with God," and he was left with a limp.

Losing the self we thought we had, being defeated: When I sit zazen my mind (my identity) keeps coming back, creating thoughts again and again, and something else releases those thoughts. This is about giving up the work of insisting that I exist. It's allowing myself to be temporary, fragile, changing, created moment by moment; there is the action of zazen. We need to lose that wrestling match.

Who plays? The small child with no obligations or duties. And the one who is not afraid. The discovery of rattlesnakes in the blackberry fields almost destroyed our play. Yes, we then wore rubber boots to protect ourselves, and we learned to make noise and to look down. And that made the time less joyful. Bringing berries back for the family, for pies and cobblers and eating and jam, that had never interfered with play at all.

Zazen is play, and the structure of reality is different in play. It's not brutal. It's not full of rules, except laws of gravity and physics like falling hurts and ice is cold.

I want to talk about changing the structure of reality.

The first thing is that, to a large extent, we create that structure. Not completely. But zazen changes the shape of our minds, so it changes our creation. This is easy to understand even if confusing. What Im offering here is that zazen does more than that personal change. Im imagining that when I sit quietly maybe say when I enter the stillness of samadhi, which is sometimes called a moment of enlightenment when the mutual

OPEN REALITY

co-creating of everything becomes real to me, the structure of reality looks like that mutual process.

Heres the other part: Dogen says that when we sit silently in samadhi, we become one with that interdependent co-creation. We are throwing our open and luminous stillness into the creation of everything. I assert that this has an effect on the way the world works, and the kind of effect is not like "I have more money" or "I have love." Maybe its like lubricating the gears on a car, so they work more smoothly. Or releasing tight muscles, so the body moves more easily.

So many of the Buddhist chants claiming magical powers are chants of gratitude and praise. People from other religions attest to the same: Gratitude is a root source. Gratitude restructures the world.

For millennia people lived lives immersed in nature and the sacred. This was true in the times of gathering and hunting, of nomadic pastoralists and small farmers. There is power in that connection. Just as deep meditation changes you and thus also your community, communal joy and ritual transform a people.

The community that dedicates its energy to the sacred is a community with the power of life.

We can find our way back and forward, we can connect again with the earth and her spirits, and we can reach both the depth and the power held there.

I propose to you that what worked for thousands of years could work again—not in some magical way but as the power of life, like the power of a healthy immune system to defeat infection.

And I propose that we begin to act as they did. Recognize the earth as our home and all beings as our family. Treat them well, work for their well-being, and partner with them in the common cause of the well-being of the Biosystem, of all of us and each of us. Join the Alliance that both defends and restores Life.

Make offerings and prayers, settle into the stillness of deep meditation, stop interfering with things as they are, place ourselves in the hands of all beings. And allow ourselves to know the more-than-joy that results.

SHODO SPRING

Gather together, to chant, drum, dance, sing in a sacred manner. Allow ourselves to be carried by the communal ecstatic ritual, released into the power of all beings.

Each group develops its own culture and style, while knowing the others are there. And together we release ourselves into the song of the earth.

INTERLUDE: SOWING CLOVER

February 2, 1968
In the dark of the moon, in flying snow,
in the dead of winter,
war spreading, families dying, the world in danger,
I walk the rocky hillside, sowing clover.

—*Wendell Berry*

One sows clover to enrich the soil, to build something for the long future. It's an act toward life in the largest sense, not tomorrow's food but a whole generation of living beings nourished, and the next generation, and the one after that.

PART 4

WHAT WE DO NOW

"I wish it need not have happened in my time," said Frodo.

"So do I," said Gandalf, "and so do all who live to see such times. But that is not for them to decide. All we have to decide is what to do with the time that is given us."

—J.R.R. Tolkien, *The Lord of the Rings*

TWENTY-ONE

TAKING OUR PLACES

Here we are. Inescapably.

Around us, and within us, there is chaos, division, anger, fear, madness. People refusing to speak to each other, arguing true and false, enemy and friend, right and wrong. There is also love, rebellion, creativity, inspiration, commitment, and a whole world of possibilities.

The place beyond right and wrong is where we can meet. As Rumi said:

> Out beyond ideas of wrongdoing and right doing
> there is a field. I will meet you there.
> When the soul lies down in that grass,
> the world is too full to talk about.
> Ideas, language, even the phrase each other
> doesn't make any sense.[i]

Let us begin by finding that place, the calm place. In Zen we say "the study of the Way," and that study is a way of life. Entering the Way, we become free, and that allows us to be calm and stable when needed. The mind doubts the possibility, but living in the Way brings it forth.

SHODO SPRING

Letting Ourselves Be Created

I, you, this person, any person is neither permanent nor independent. Thats a strange thought, but its also intuitively obvious: Im different today from who I was yesterday, and this evening when I gather with friends Ill be someone else yet. This person is created both by everyone I meet, both human and nonhuman, and by my past actions, words, and thoughts. We call it the "true human body." It means being a participant in the life of the world, a creator and created at the same time, recreated every moment. My teacher wrote once:

> Our lives are patterns of the fabric produced by the loom of time and space.
> When we see the individual things, each one is impermanent, constantly changing, without any fixed independent entity. But this work of weaving continues. Our life is a result and a gift from people and things from the past.
> What we do now influences later generations, whether positively or negatively. The loom is weaving the ancient brocade of eternity, while the spring is new, fresh and different each year.
> The spring of the entire heaven and earth is manifested within a tiny plum blossom in the cold air. The tiny blossom actualizes the spring of the entire heaven and earth.
> All individual things are working together as a whole without anything being excluded. There is no observer and observation from outside.

> —Shohaku Okumura

Foundations

My house is immovable. slept in it through giant storms—including one that pushed rain through the edges of perfectly good windows—and nothing shook. Nothing moved. The storm woke me, but the house was rock solid. Concrete block the whole first level, plus another four feet below the basement, with footers anchoring the extra four feet. Wind slides over the barn roof instead of catching and shaking it.

OPEN REALITY

In the 2019 tornado, the only thing that happened to this house was that the vent blew off the chimney—while trees crashed everywhere around. In this house, my body is at ease.

Might it be possible to live in a mind that won't shake or crumble in a storm?

I don't know every way to enter such a mind. I know one: the practice of zazen (see Chapter 20). We sit comfortably erect, and refrain from physical movement. When thoughts come up, we release them. We allow the present to exist, in pleasure or discomfort, and our mind to gradually settle. Thoughts clamor "me, me" or "warning, warning" or "outrage" or any other such thing. We allow them to slide up and over and past, without shaking us. And when shaken, we allow the emotion to slide also.

Years of such practice creates a foundation that rests quietly without disturbance. That can endure tornadoes. That can thus become a shelter.

Another practice is that of community. Spiritual community, based on shared intention to deepen and open in this way. Practical community, doing a work together. Nourishing community, tending each other and also playing together. Ecstatic community, deeply bonded by knowing the sacred together in our bodies. These communities will include some humans and perhaps some others animals, trees, berry bushes, the creek, the grasses.

In my own dreams, a local or even residential community can support each other in all of these ways. Community can think together, "What needs to happen now?", "Who has what gifts that respond to this emergency?" and "How can the rest of us support that response?"

The work to do cannot be completely internal or psychological. Being created by everything in the world, even though we feel like individuals we are responsible to that world. Each community is mutually created, each creates its collective response. Life comes forth in those actions.

In Zen, "Studying the Way" or "Practicing the Way" includes listening to everything and everyone around us, deeply listening, receiving,

SHODO SPRING

allowing ourselves to be created. Theres a security in that beyond anything we could make by force or intention.

Ask for Help

A tragedy of this age is how we've thought ourselves alone. As individuals, families, towns, workplaces, states, nations, or the human species, we've imagined ourselves separate and independent. Thus we've been unable to imagine help from spirits, or gods or God, we've not asked help from forests even while our scientists describe the many ways forests help all of those within them.

Relying only on ourselves, we've damaged the others who might have helped us. Who have been helping us all along. The deep wilderness is the vital heart and soul of the whole of Earth, the entire Biosystem. Rather than logging and mining, we could return to worshiping. Listening. Receiving. Meditating there. Making offerings. Ceremony. Humility. Prayer. Gratitude. And faith.

Vow

> *Go ahead,*
> *light your candles, burn your incense,*
> *ring your bells and call out to the Gods*
>
> *but watch out,*
> *because the Gods will come.*
> *And they will put you on the anvil*
> *and fire up the forge*
> *and beat you and beat you until they turn brass into pure gold.*[ii]

TWENTY-TWO
A PROMISE OF HELP

Its not often that I hear voices. When they speak, I listen. This is an attempt to describe a time out of ordinary reality. It makes no rational sense, but something changed in me.

In May of 2023, I was at a retreat, surrounded by people who understood the relationship between humans and nature, and settling in with them, to have finally found my people in a group called Kincentric Leadership. Friday was the day of the solo, alone in the wilderness for a spiritual engagement that would be different for each of us.

For a week we'd been immersed in community, in practices and learnings fostering deep connection with the natural world, several hours each day outdoors in sun and shade, together or alone. The day before had been wholly dedicated to ritual preparing for the solo, including finding the spot where each of us would spend several hours. I'd found a rocky outcrop, not far from the lodge, just above the road, and facing the Continental Divide. I spent time there, explored the area, identified a possible refuge for bad weather, then meditated and chanted. Well, not exactly. Actually, I sang and shouted with whole body and mind, taken over as the energy streamed through. Late afternoon, I tore myself away from the magic, promising to return.

On Friday morning we gathered with ceremony, then set out each for our place. The morning was sunny, and rain was promised. I had just enough gear

SHODO SPRING

to stay warm and dry—hopefully—and some survival food. I checked in with my refuge place, positioned my extra clothes to soften the bumpy rock, and settled in facing the mountains.

Little memory remains. The sky was clear over the mountains to the south. Clouds came in gradually, then winds. Shadows moved in over the mountains, then winds, then rain—while I sat in sunlight. As the hours passed, I added clothing, one piece at a time. The thought "Thunder beings" came to mind. "I've been neglecting the thunder beings." My long affinity with the thunder beings had suddenly returned after years of forgetting. The storm came closer, and I just watched with all my senses. My whole body shakes now, as I reach for memories gone beyond thoughts.

It was darker, and colder, and windier. I walked a bit to stretch, then settled in for the storm, wearing every bit of clothing and the rain poncho on top. Wind. Cold. Dark. The hail came, pounding down on my hat, gathering on the poncho and on the rocks around me. I drew everything close, and was grateful to be dry. An infinite time passed. I was afraid of the cold. I drank water and ate bits of food to hold me.

I can't exactly tell you what happened in that time beyond the ordinary world. Seeking words, I'll call it a wrestling match with the great primordial powers and particularly the Thunder Beings. Not to win or lose, but to enter the grand alliance that has been calling to me.

Now and then my reasonable mind would ask whether I needed to come down the rocky path before it became dangerous. It was met by an unreasonable longing to stay until I could bask in the sun right there facing the mountains. I stayed. Eventually the sun did come out, and warmth came back, and even though there was rain and melted hail, my wish came true.

When I finally came down the hill, it was not as a human or a self, but as just part of the whole living thing. It was intensely private. Back at the lodge, I hid to avoid speaking. Even now, in order to write I have to call my own words a sacred ritual.

Sometime during the hail, the message had come. "The Thunder Beings have promised to help." Every part of me knew it was true. That evening, after quiet sharing in twos and threes, those were my words to the group. They are my

OPEN REALITY

words to the world, to everyone who is caught in the tension between hope and fear. We don't have to do it alone. We are helped by very powerful forces.

This could only happen in context. I was surrounded by human beings in Kincentric Leadership, in the commitment to work with and within the natural world and the human world, where relationship is the center. It matters that I was on holy land. It matters that I live in the vow. And help offered itself.

AFTERWORD: SACRED PRACTICE

Today, in the sunlight and cold, with light glistening off the snow and drops of water falling from icicles, as the figs bear their new-hoped fruit in the eastern window, today I walked down to the Central Altar, to the place where spirits look out from the rock wall. The old grandmother was there, with Wolf looking out over her right eye, and the dark meditating woman and the one on horseback who then turned into a dancing woman with another ghostlike figure dancing next to her. They come and go, depending on the time of day, how the shadows fall, and perhaps the welcome in my mind. Today to the right was a large dark shield, with a few human faces turned to the east new to me and to the left a standing figure who reminded me of images of Jesus. The crowds were there in the lower center, as usual, looking up toward the larger figures.

With tobacco in my bare cold hand, I spoke a few words. Then I chanted the *Dai Hi Shin Dharani*, dharani of great compassion, the very old magical chant offered daily in Soto Zen temples around the world. After chanting we dedicate the merit, the positive energy, to good and worthy causes. I asked for a few things, for the lands up north, and for these beings here.

Just briefly, the bald eagle came by.

AFTERWORD: SACRED PRACTICE

If you close your eyes, you can feel the energy of land and creek, rocks and bluffs, grasses and red cedar trees, blue sky and snow, all of it together.

I'm just beginning to share this practice with other humans. Some aspects of it have been given already, for others I'm still in training, and in the past year I have found so many people who are ahead of me on this road. There will be work with the hands, in woods, fields, and garden; and there will be shared ritual work—in any sacred place, perhaps by the river or on top of the bluff, in the meadow or in the woods, or even at Shovel Point on the shores of Lake Superior. The time is close.

This is our work at Mountains and Waters Alliance. It's not that we disappear into the woods or never engage with city life again, and certainly not that we ignore the confrontation between earth protectors and captains of industry. It's that, in the middle of all that, we are nourished by the many beings and we make offerings to them. Sitting meditation, yes, and walking, and letting our bodies rest between earth and sky. Learning to listen, until we won't harvest a stick of wood or pull a dandelion without a certain sense of willingness, of rightness, of welcome from the family of that stick or this dandelion. There's a long slowing-down that allows us to settle into belonging. The next movement arises from that.

There are practices, with the earth family or together with human community, that can help this slowing down, opening, breathing in life and the long mourning of every leaf and fallen stone, every brittle grass and broken tree, and the eternal joy in the rippling of water over stone and rustling of wind in white pine trees and the call of the mourning dove in the spring. A few are mentioned here and there in the book. For now, pause one moment and inhabit your skin.

In the long-term dream, we sense each other, small or large groups all around the earth, and go to the sacred spaces closest to us, and make offerings, of beauty and music and dance, of silence and witness. Our intention is simply blessing, whatever words we may put on it. Each gathering finds its own way, in stillness or movement, silence or sound, words or just voice.

AFTERWORD: SACRED PRACTICE

In my near-term imagining, we come to know each other, we use internet and telephone and speak friend-to-friend; we name a date when we will join, each in our own places, and each group finds its own way. Like a thousand flowers, each circle blooms in the languages and ceremonies that belong to its own place and the humans who come. None are the same tongue, and all are a shared heart.

Then the Alliance is manifest: mountains and waters, forests and marshes and deserts and oceans, microbes and fungi, mice and deer and spiders and hawks, humans of all kinds, and a great energy rises up.

I dare to say it is possible this alliance may heal the damage in our world. I'm certain it can heal our hearts.

APPENDIX 1: REWRITING A HISTORY THAT IS FALSE

Early Ancestors

I stated that our ideas of how the ancestors lived are too simplistic and too uniform; I promised to say more.

Our idea of the classic hunter-gatherer pattern is narrow. Here are a few known variations. One style: In summer, small bands roamed the land, hunting and foraging and developing the land to such an extent that you might accurately say "food forest gardening." In winter, people gathered in larger settlements and practiced ritual and ceremony, sometimes with an intensely structured life including roles and hierarchies.

Another pattern: Some groups gathered in summer and dispersed in fall. North American examples of this pattern were the Mandan-Hidatsa and the Crow, both former farming groups who had changed to a primarily nomadic life. They would congregate for the buffalo hunt, appointing a temporary police force with strong powers, and then split up again after the hunt and the following Sun Dance. In short, they rotated between small bands and a powerful State, on the opposite cycle from the first group. Graeber and Wengrow summarize anthropologist Lowies observations thus:

APPENDIX 1: REWRITING A HISTORY THAT IS FALSE

> *They were conscious political actors, keenly aware of the possibil-*
> *ities and dangers of authoritarian power. Not only did they*
> *dismantle all means of exercising coercive authority the moment*
> *the ritual season was over, they were also careful to rotate which*
> *clan or warrior clubs got to wield it: Anyone holding sovereignty*
> *one year would be subject to the authority of others in the next.*[i]

Other gathering-hunting societies that don't fit narrow expectations include the Kwakiutl of the Pacific Northwest and some ice age hunter-gatherer societies including Dolni Vestonice, Gobekli Tepe, Yudinovo, Mezhirich and Kostenki. These had majestic monuments, ornate individual burials, and the like, but no evidence of the fortifications or storehouses which would indicate a settled society. Descriptions of them are found throughout Graeber and Wengrows *The Dawn of Everything*, particularly in Chapter 3. They quote French anthropologist Pierre Clastres:

> *What if the sort of people we like to imagine as simple and inno-*
> *cent are free of rulers, governments, bureaucracies, ruling classes*
> *and the like, not because they are lacking in imagination, but*
> *because they're actually more imaginative than we are? We find*
> *it difficult to picture what a truly free society would be like;*
> *perhaps they have no similar trouble picturing what arbitrary*
> *power and domination would be like. Perhaps they can not only*
> *imagine it, but consciously arrange their society in such a way as*
> *to avoid it.*

And they add:

> *By insisting that the people studied by anthropologists are just as*
> *self-conscious, just as aware, as the anthropologists themselves,*
> *[Clastres] did more to reverse the damage than anyone before or*
> *since.*[ii]

In other words, maybe those people lived in egalitarian ways because they had figured out how to create a free society? Also, they were able to combine freedom with unequal wealth; wealth might give responsibility

APPENDIX 1: REWRITING A HISTORY THAT IS FALSE

but it did not give power. Many chiefs led only by the power of persuasion, without any enforcement ability. In two additional examples, we note that consensus decision-making was not considered unusual in early Buddhist sanghas (monastic communities), and in modern Bali, people of all castes meet together to make decisions.[iii]

Throughout known history, past and present, people have designed communities intended to work in egalitarian ways, from Europes medieval Diggers to Indias Auroville now.

When Europeans Encounter Indigenous Wisdom

In the sixteenth century, the ideas of indigenous American philosophers came to Europe and were widely acclaimed as rational and reasonable, competing successfully with the previously-dominant religious thought. For example, the Wendat philosopher-statesman Kandiaronk was quoted and widely read through his dialogues with a French aristocrat who called himself Lahontan:

> *I find it hard to see how you could be much more miserable than you already are. What kind of human, what species of creature, must Europeans be, that they have to be forced to do good, and only refrain from evil because of fear of punishment? ...*
> *You have observed that we lack judges. What is the reason for that? Well, we never bring lawsuits against one another. And why do we never bring lawsuits? Well, because we made a decision neither to accept or make use of money. And why do we refuse to allow money into our communities? The reason is this: We are determined not to have laws because, since the world was a world, our ancestors have been able to live contentedly without them.*[iv]

Their dialogues were translated into German, English, Dutch, and Italian, and remained in print for over a century. Kandiaronk had observed the colonial settlers and had also visited Europe. Open discussion, collective decision-making, philosophical debate, and female authority were common in the Americas, and seem to have been very attractive to Europeans who read about them. A battle of ideas followed in European mainstream thought. A.R.J. Turgot claimed that equality is only possible

APPENDIX 1: REWRITING A HISTORY THAT IS FALSE

where everyone is equally poor, and that different abilities naturally lead to complex societies in which poverty is a necessary part.[v] He offered a paradigm of evolution from primitive to advanced, that "usual story" I mentioned in Chapter 4. Because that idea persists, I offer a few examples of exceptions to Turgot's analysis:

Cities[vi]

We commonly associate cities with hierarchy and inequality. Yet, just as some hunter-gatherer peoples had temporary hierarchies, some cities were egalitarian. Ancient Mesopotamian cities seem to have been designed for near-universal participation in governing: Before 3200 BCE Uruk had great public assembly halls and courts for gatherings, much like ancient Athens. Arslantepe in eastern Turkey was similar, until its temple was replaced by a palace plus weapons, suggesting the beginning of what is called "heroic society." The heroic societies were oligarchies; they acquired wealth but did not accumulate it, rather spending or giving it away. They resisted writing and commerce. Many parts of the Near East show mixed-gender town councils, citizen assemblies and councils of elders, lots of freedom and little slavery.

In ancient Ukraine and Moldova, cities appeared with no evidence of either centralized government or ruling class. Similar houses are arranged in circles around an open center whose uses are unclear. These people gardened, foraged, and hunted, extracted flint, made ceramics, and imported salt and copper. There was surplus but no evidence of warfare or elites. Women may have held leadership or simply high status. Even though these held thousands of residents, modern archaeologists refer to them as megasites rather than cities. Minoan Crete also seems to have had a society without war, apparently with woman leadership, until conquered by the Greeks about 1400 BCE.

Why Don't We Know About This?

Apparently its too hard to believe. Graeber and Wengrow note the scholarly assumption of authoritarian institutions:

> Scholars tend to demand clear and irrefutable evidence for the existence of democratic institutions of any sort in the distant past. It's striking how they never demand comparably rigorous proof

108

APPENDIX 1: REWRITING A HISTORY THAT IS FALSE

for top-down structures of authority. These latter are usually treated as a default mode of history: the kind of social structures you would simply expect to see in the absence of evidence for anything else.[vii]

General public opinion is shaped by that assumption. Other ways of living are considered unrealistic or utopian, though examples continue to arise in settled and "civilized" societies of many times.

APPENDIX 2: TRUE REPORTS OF WHAT PEOPLE ARE LIKE

If we think humans are inherently evil, we'll make decisions based on that, and the whole culture becomes problematic. Thus I offer some corrective tales from Rutger Bregman.

Stories

The 1954 novel *Lord of the Flies* was famous while I was in college in the late 1960s. I tried to read it but couldn't bear it. Like everyone, though, I knew its message: People are bad, deep down. This bit of fiction has come to be read and taught as "a harsh look into what kids are really like," an exploration of human nature and why we need to be controlled.

The Stanford Prison Experiment, 1971, was intended to lead to prison reform. Famously, in an experiment making some college students guards and the others prisoners, the guards became so sadistic that they had to call off the experiment after six days. The message is still taught: Ordinary people easily become sadists. It must be our nature.

The Stanley Milgram experiments attempted to understand how the Nazis could do what they did. He found that Americans too were willing to give painful and even fatal shocks to other people. In 1961 they did the experiment with 500 male subjects; later experiments

APPENDIX 2: TRUE REPORTS OF WHAT PEOPLE ARE LIKE

involved women and other groups. The message? Deep down, we're all Nazis. We must be controlled.

Kitty Genovese, 1964. A woman was stabbed to death with dozens of people watching, nobody even called the police, and she died alone on the sidewalk. For years, you could say "Kitty Genovese" and everyone knew you meant "Nobody cares. You are alone. Nobody will help."[i] I remember the fear this brought me as a sixteen-year-old girl.

Stories like these have shaped our shared understanding. Decisions are made based on the notion that human nature is like this. It's worth looking at them carefully.

Lord of the Flies: In the time when that novel was revered as telling deep and terrible truths about human nature, Danish historian Rutger Bregman went looking for a true story that would teach something different. He found it. Six boys had been shipwrecked on a rocky islet south of Tonga in June 1965 and rescued by an Australian sea captain in September 1966. They'd run away from St. Andrew's boarding school, stealing a fishing boat and hoping to sail to Fiji on a lark. Instead, they crashed on 'Ata and made a life there for fifteen months. They didn't enjoy it, they just did it. They didn't hurt each other. They cooperated, they kept the signal fire going, and when one broke a leg the others tended him to complete recovery.

There were attempts to replicate *Lord of the Flies* with real kids. Here's one of many: The Robbers Cave Experiment, 1954. Two groups of eleven-year-old boys were taken to a beautiful park and allowed to do whatever they wanted. In the second week a competition between the groups included burning a flag and looting comic books. The researcher notes that the kids opposed the competition. "Maybe we could make friends with those guys," one boy suggested. Bregman cites other research attempts to get boys to behave badly, all unsuccessful.[ii]

The Stanford Prison Experiment: The guards were selected for sadistic tendencies, then continuously pressured to inflict more cruelty "for the sake of the research." I wonder what the guards thought when they learned they were actually the subjects of the research. Apparently you actually have to select guards for sadism, and then push them to cruelty.

APPENDIX 2: TRUE REPORTS OF WHAT PEOPLE ARE LIKE

You'd think that would have been enough to make some changes in prison structure. The point of the experiment was to reform prisons.

The British Prison Experiment, 2001, went quite differently, and was discontinued because nothing happened except guards sharing food with prisoners, "Let's discuss this like human beings," a democracy, an escape to go smoke with the guards, a vote to create a commune.

For TV producers, the experiment exposed a harsh truth: If you leave ordinary people alone, nothing happens. Or worse, they'll try to start a pacifist commune. The researchers published more than ten articles about their results, but the study faded into obscurity after demonstrating that people are not brutal and evil. [iii]

The Stanley Milgram experiments supposedly showed that ordinary people were willing to torture and kill innocent people by electric shock. When the archives were studied, it turned out that "Anyone who deviated from his script was brought to heel by the application of intense pressure. ... 'The slavish obedience to authority,' writes Gina Perry, 'comes to sound much more like bullying and coercion when you listen to these recordings [of the research process].'" In addition, "His archives are filled with statements from participants expressing doubt." In both the original experiment and in later copies, as soon as an actual order is given (to continue the shocks), every subject refuses. The more overbearing the instructor became, the more the subjects defied orders.

Ordinary people are better than we think.

Kitty Genovese: Above is a bit of the newspaper story. Actually, first a neighbor shouted at the assailant, who went away but then came back to kill her. Second, there were multiple calls to the police, who ignored them. Third, the "thirty-eight witnesses who didn't do anything" included everyone who lived on that street, most of whom couldn't have heard anything. Last, a friend who was a gay man (in a time when being gay could cost your life) did find a friend of Kittys, who went to her and held her. Kitty did not die alone and unloved. Bregman's story goes into more detail; the history.com story is basic, but mentions the misleading press. (See note i.)

APPENDIX 2: TRUE REPORTS OF WHAT PEOPLE ARE LIKE

Sociableness

People are naturally sociable. This has several effects. One effect is that we learn from each other. Another is that, in order to protect those they love, humans will go to any lengths including hurting and killing others. Brian Hare and Vanessa Woods write:

> *The best way to diffuse conflict among groups is to diminish the perceived sense of threat through social interaction. If feeling threatened makes us want to protect others in our group, nonthreatening contact between groups allows us to expand the definition of who our group is.*
> *Most policies are enacted with the assumption that a change in attitude will lead to a change in behavior, but in the case of inter-group conflict, it is the altered behavior—in the form of human contact—that will most likely change minds.*
> *A change in behavior produces changes in attitude. People who work together, go to school together, or share neighborhood events, come to recognize each other as part of their group who should be defended rather than a danger who should be attacked.*[iv]

Its deeply relevant that human beings are not essentially as mean and selfish as we have been made out to be. We probably will help our immediate neighbors, and they will most likely help us, in an actual emergency.

In traditional life, there are ways to grow a community that does whats needed. Martín Prechtel describes one of these:

> *The secret of village togetherness and happiness has always been the generosity of the people, but the key to that generosity is inefficiency and decay. Because our village huts were not built to last very long, they had to be regularly renewed. To do this, villagers came together, at least once a year, to work on somebody's hut. When your house was falling down, you invited all the folks over. The little kids ran around messing up what everybody was doing. The young women brought the water. The young men carried the stones. The older men told everybody what to do, and the older*

APPENDIX 2: TRUE REPORTS OF WHAT PEOPLE ARE LIKE

women told the older men that they weren't doing it right. Once the house was back together again, everyone ate together, praised the house, laughed, and cried. In a few days, they moved on to the next house. In this way, each family's place in the village was reestablished and remembered. This is how it always was.

Then the missionaries and the businessmen and the politicians brought in tin and lumber and sturdy houses. Now the houses last, but the relationships don't.

In resistance camps across Turtle Island (North America), a great learning is happening. Watching from the sidelines, I see people taking care of food and shelter in the middle of running civil resistance and education and legal actions. The example I know the best is at the Line 3 pipeline resistance in northern Minnesota.[v] Somebody organizes food, shelter, health and medical care, along with speakers, microphones, publicity, action plan, education, everything you can think of.

Thats in the past now. The camp remains, doing cultural activities. In fall 2023 I went to a wild ricing camp. I don't know what I expected, but what I found was community. And in a quiet conversation, a woman organizer told me they intended to do activities for healing the trauma of those who had resisted. The people who had sacrificed individually for the common good were suffering individually from trauma: physical injury, arrest, jail, brutality, and more. A community needs to take care of its own.[vi]

LIFE-AFFIRMING RESOURCES

This is not just a list of books, but a list of resources, including people and organizations who are doing great work.

The list is short; many more valuable resources are in the footnotes. Its purpose is to offer relevant material, which I've read, about which I can say without hesitation: It is worth your while to read every one of these books.

People and Organizations

Mountains and Waters Alliance, https://mountainsandwatersalliance.org/. I founded this organization after an encounter with plants and hills where I live. I had asked them to protect themselves from development, and they did; more, they spoke to me through every cell of my body. Our intention is to create a worldwide community of people in local groups, who listen, make offerings, and take action based on teachings from plants, animals, rivers, mountains, all the wisdom-keepers and power-holders of the natural world. As we develop, others are doing similar things.

Kincentric Leadership, https://www.kincentricleadership.org/about-kincentric-leadership, no books yet. Founded by Justine Huxley and Anna Kovasna in 2022, they speak of "weaving humanity back into the

LIFE-AFFIRMING RESOURCES

web of life." I'm part of this group, which is currently creating itself through a worldwide web of retreats and online training and connections.

Resilience, https://www.resilience.org/, is a library, a public square, an educational resource, articles and podcasts, and seminars oriented toward increasing community resilience in the context of climate change, pollution, dependence on fossil fuels, and other influences today.

The Design Pathway for Regenerating Earth https://design-school-for-regenerating-earth.mn.co/ (Earth Regenerators Press, 2021). Founded by Joe Brewer, they are actually working to restore the earth, by bioregions, informed by indigenous and nature-led wisdom, including an online school and projects in some places.

Global Evergreening Alliance, https://www.evergreening.org/. Massive land restoration projects. My connection there is Phyllis Barnard, co-author of "Earth at Risk: an urgent call to end the age of destruction and forge a just and sustainable future." https://academic.oup.com/pnas nexus/article/3/4/pgae106/7638480

Bayo Akolomafe, https://www.bayoakomolafe.net/, showed up in my awareness a few years ago. His writing is always profound and challenging. I find it impossible to translate his wild poetic expressions into rational language, but I recognize that we are going in the same direction. Go wander around his website. Something new is happening here.

Regi Haslett-Marroquin, https://www.regenagalliance.org/farmers/salvatierra-farms/, started as a boy farming in Guatamala, now inspiring and decolonizing regenerative agriculture around the world. This short talk gives a clue of his thinking: https://www.youtube.com/watch?v=UxzE-fDHN3g

Sacred Mountain Sangha, founded by Thanissara and Kittisaro, www.sacredmountainsangha.org. "This is the decade where we decide if we collectively evolve into the higher dream of humanity or devolve into a path toward extinction."

LIFE-AFFIRMING RESOURCES

One Earth Sangha, https://oneearthsangha.org/about-us/ "The mission of One Earth Sangha is to support humanity in a transformative response to ecological crises based on the insights and practices of the Buddhist tradition."

More such organizations are born every day.

Books

If you were moved by this book and want to go deeper, I recommend reading any or every book on this short list. Its limited by a few factors: I've read them. They're highly relevant to this work. They're mostly recent. More are being written every day.

Abram, David. *The Spell of the Sensuous: Perception and Language in a More-Than-Human World*. New York, Random House, 1996. Writing after fieldwork in Bali, Abram proposes that "we are human only in contact, and conviviality, with what is not human." And he makes it easy to imagine.

Armstrong, Karen. *The Great Transformation: The Beginning of Our Religious Traditions*. New York: Anchor Books, 2007. Armstrong offers a steady historical sense of the transitions and peoples who birthed the religions we have today.

Berman, Morris. *Wandering God: A Study in Nomadic Spirituality*. Albany: State University of New York Press, 2000. Berman is a historian and social critic; this book investigates cultural and spiritual ways of being, and applies that study to what we might do now.

Bregman, Rutger. *Humankind: A Hopeful History,* tr. Manton and Moore. New York: Little, Brown and Company, 2019. Danish historian Bregman removes the negative lens with which we view our fellow humans, offering data to challenge stories that "prove" we are inherently selfish and evil.

Hedges, Christopher. *War Is a Force That Gives Us Meaning*. New York: Public Affairs, 2002. After years as a war correspondent,

LIFE-AFFIRMING RESOURCES

Hedges wrote about the reality of war. All his books and talks are fierce; this one is also very human and deeply insightful about humans in war.

Macy, Joanna, and Molly Brown. *Coming Back to Life: The Updated Guide to the Work That Reconnects*, New Society Publishers, 2014. The book opens with an intimate and compelling invitation into the understanding that guides this work. It continues as a training manual for those who would share the healing work with communities. The whole is inspiring.

Curtis, Adam. "BBC Four Documentaries — The Century of the Self" BBC Online. This series vividly portrays how modern consumer culture was deliberately created over the past hundred years to create a citizenry easily manipulated, and how that manipulation entered the political world. https://www.youtube.com/watch?v=GFwDc17WZ-A Archived from the original on May 14, 2011.

Donaldson, O. Fred. *Playing by Heart: The Vision and Practice of Belonging*. Deerfield Beach, Florida: Health Communications, 1993. Donaldson addresses the difference between competitive play and natural play, with vivid examples. He teaches "original play" through an organization, https://originalplay.eu/.

Ehrenreich, Barbara. *Dancing in the Streets*: *A History of Collective Joy*. New York: Henry Holt & Co, 2007. I was looking for more information about how our culture lost its spiritual joy and found this book describing both that joy and its suppression.

Ereira, Alan. *From the Heart of the World – The Elder Brothers Warning* (1992) and *Aluna* (2018). Both available online, on Youtube. The Kogi people, who lived in seclusion for centuries, called BBC filmmaker Ereira to convey their message, twice.

Forbes, Jack D. *Columbus and Other Cannibals: The Wetiko Disease of Exploitation, Imperialism, and Terrorism, revised edition.* New York, Seven Stories Press, 1992 and 2008. Forbes defines wetiko in connec-

LIFE-AFFIRMING RESOURCES

tion with the colonizing Europeans, after first offering a vivid description of indigenous ways of thought.

Gagliano, Monica. *Thus Spoke the Plant: A Remarkable Journey of Groundbreaking Scientific Discoveries and Personal Encounters With Plants*. Berkeley: North Atlantic Books, 2018. This book vividly shows the power of plants. The author also has several videos on YouTube.

Graeber, David and David Wengrow. *The Dawn of Everything: A New History of Humanity*. New York: Farrar, Straus and Giroux, 2021. This massive work challenges what we thought we knew about history and our ancestors, and opens the door to new possibilities.

Illich, Ivan. *ABC: The Alphabetization of the Popular Mind*. New York: Vintage Books, 1989. More on the flattening of our minds and cultures.

Jacobs, Jane. *Cities and the Wealth of Nations: Principles of Economic Life*. New York: Vintage Books, 1985. Jacobs discusses both the liveliness and the harms of cities. My favorite of her many books.

Jensen, Derrick. *Endgame Volume II: Resistance*. New York: Seven Stories Press, 2006. This was my introduction to Jensens work. Here he asks the question of why we don't protect life. I find his work well researched and deeply joyful, even as he takes on the most difficult topics.

Kimmerer, Robin Wall. *Braiding Sweetgrass: Indigenous Wisdom, Scientific Knowledge, and the Teachings of Plants*. Minneapolis: Milkweed Editions, 2013. Kimmerer offers an image of a way of life. She also has many recorded video talks.

Kogi see Ereira.

Lamoreux, M. Lynn. *Saving Life*. Bloomington, Indiana: Authorhouse, 2021. Clear and careful discussion of systems, biology, and other science for the purpose of sharing "a sustainable world view true to the nature of Life." By a retired geneticist.

LIFE-AFFIRMING RESOURCES

Lamoreux, Lynn, and Dorothy Bennett. 2024. "Scientists Warning on the Problem With Overpopulation and Living Systems" *The Journal of Population and Sustainability* 8 (1):95-111. https://www.whp-journals. co.uk/JPS/article/view/997/693. This concisely discusses the same topics as the 2021 Lamoreux book, with focus on population as a key issue. The references constitute an excellent reading list for science on the topic.

Loy, David. *Ecodharma: Buddhist Teachings for the Ecological Crisis.* Somerville: Wisdom Publications, 2018. This is a core text on Buddhism and environmentalism.

Mayer, Milton. *They Thought They Were Free: The Germans, 1933-45.* Chicago: The University of Chicago Press, published 1954, 1966 and 2017. Mayer lived in Germany for a year after the end of World War II, and reports from interviews with ten people who joined the Nazi party, with context.

Mathews, Freya. *Reinhabiting Reality: Towards a Recovery of Culture.* Albany: State University of New York Press, 2005.

Miller, Asher, and Richard Heinberg. *Welcome to the Great Unraveling: Navigating the Polycrisis of Environmental and Social Breakdown,* https://www.postcarbon.org/publications/welcome-to-the-great-unraveling/, 2023. This is a thorough and comprehensive overview of collapse. It details economic, resource, social, and economic causes and effects, dispelling common illusions. Moving on to what can be done, they begin with obstacles to systemic change (biophysical realities, cognitive bias, entrenched socioeconomic and belief systems, and "diminished capacity to act systemically or pro-socially,") investigating each in detail. Finally, "what you can do" as an individual addresses ways of thinking, the meaning of personal resilience, and specific steps including building community and connecting with the more-than-human world. It would be a great preliminary to reading *Open Reality.*

Myers, Natasha. *How to grow liveable worlds: Ten (not-so-easy) steps for life in the Planthroposcene,* January 28, 2020, in *ABC Religion and*

LIFE-AFFIRMING RESOURCES

Ethics, https://www.abc.net.au. Instructions for the life that could change us.

Narby, Jeremy. *The Cosmic Serpent: DNA and the Origins of Knowledge.* New York: TarcherPerigree, 1999. Investigating traditional knowledge of psychedelic plants.

Orion, Tao. *Beyond the War on Invasive Species: A Permaculture Approach to Ecosystem Restoration.* White River Junction: Chelsea Green Publishing, 2015. The title says everything. How do we stop warring on the natural world? Includes a science-based exploration of why that war doesn't work.

Patel, Raj, and Jason W. Moore. *History of the World in Seven Cheap Things: A Guide to Capitalism, Nature, and the Future of the Planet.* Oakland: University of California Press, 2017. As the title says.

Prechtel, Martin. *The Unlikely Peace at Cuchumaquic: The Parallel Lives of People as Plants: Keeping the Seeds Alive.* Berkeley: North Atlantic Books, 2012. Prechtel was a Mayan shaman for ten years and then went back to the United States to teach. He writes vividly; this book in particular includes instructions for nonnative people seeking to reclaim our connection with the plant-spirit world.

Quinn, Daniel. *Ishmael: A Novel.* New York: Bantam Books, 1992. Quinns work offers attractive alternatives to common assumptions about humanity, in the pretense of a novel. *Ishmael* is where that begins, while the sequels continue it.

Sale, Kirkpatrick. *The Conquest of Paradise: Christopher Columbus and the Columbian Legacy.* New York: Penguin Books, 1991. The main gift of this book for me was its look at the European culture that launched Columbus, helping with my persistent question, "How did Europeans get so crazy?"

Snyder, Timothy. *On Tyranny: 20 Lessons from the 20th Century.* New York: Crown Publishing, 2017. Historian and expert on Eastern Europe,

LIFE-AFFIRMING RESOURCES

Snyder looks at the history of Naziism and fascism and proposes how ordinary people can slow a slide toward authoritarianism. His 2024 book *On Freedom* teaches freedom as a lively community state rather than just the absence of oppression.

Solnit, Rebecca. *A Paradise Built in Hell: The Extraordinary Communities That Arise in Disaster.* New York: Viking Penguin, 2009. Solnit documents instance after instance of people helping each other and being interrupted by government agencies meant to help.

Joseph Tainter, *The Collapse of Complex Societies,* New York: Cambridge University Press, 1988. The classic work on how and why societies destroy ourselves.

Tsing, Swanson, Gan, Bubandt, eds., *Arts of Living on a Damaged Planet: Monsters of the Anthropocene.* Minneapolis: University of Minnesota Press, 2017. This and the other Tsing book address the possible future.

Tsing, Anna. *The Mushroom at the End of the World: On the Possibility of Life in Capitalist Ruins.* Princeton: Princeton University Press, 2015. She studies the societies grown up around the matsutake mushroom in post-logging Oregon forests.

Wallace, Rob. *Dead Epidemiologists: On the Origin of COVID-19.* New York: Monthly Review Press, 2020. Wallaces careful work implicates patterns of commerce and agriculture that likely led to the start of the COVID-19 pandemic.

Work, Courtney. *Tides of Empire: Religion, Development, and Environment in Cambodia.* New York: Berghahn Books, 2020. As in all her research, Work addresses the whole picture, based on years of direct work with villagers in Cambodia plus a subtle understanding of political and economic forces in action. Access to her published work is at https://www.courtneykwork.com/.

ACKNOWLEDGMENTS

I write with gratitude for all those who nourished me along the Buddhist path, especially my transmitting teacher Shohaku Okumura;

for my readers and editors, who challenged me, encouraged me, corrected mistakes, and helped me keep going—especially Beth Goldring, Linne Jensen, Lynn Lamoreux, and Kathleen Quinn (any remaining mistakes are of course my own);

for friends with whom the conversation started thirty-some years ago: Kate Greenway, Denise Wilder, Ellen Hufschmidt, Michael MacMacha, Rachel Parker, Antiga, two women's ritual groups, and the fairy tale group; and for Martin Bulgerin and our ongoing conversation; for old colleagues and teachers in many realms: Luca Valentino, Jerry Koch-Gonzalez, Peter Bane, Keith Johnson, Paul Meyer, Ben Brabson, and others whose names disappear after all these years; for Derrick Jensen and the writing class;

for Scott Edelstein in particular, more than I can say;

for David Loy, who went first and made the road I now walk, and for befriending me;

for those who have inspired me: too many names and more added daily —look at the bibliography;

for those who walked into unknown places with me, sometimes physically, too many to name;

for my children Joy Piccolino and Robin Hackney, for their patience with my absence and strangeness;

for the Advisory Council for giving me strength and wisdom, Beth Goldring, Gareth Young, Robin Hackney, Linne Jensen, Lynn Lamoreux, Greg Colby, and former Advisor Chris Gamer;

for the spirits of the Cannon River, and the bluffs, the flowers who spoke to me on a Colorado mountain retreat, for the thunder beings who returned after I had forgotten them, for the creek of my childhood and the beaches of Lake Erie, the iris in the spring and red leaves in fall, for the waters at Gooseberry Falls and the waves of Lake Superior, the vast plains of Montana and the Appalachian spring of western Maryland, for dragonflies and wild rice and the sound of wind in trees. All these sustained me when I was lost to the human world, and they are here with me now, with us.

ABOUT THE AUTHOR

Shodo Spring has belonged to the natural world for as long as she can remember. She grew up running half-wild in the fields and woods of northeastern Ohio, with early mornings on the shore of Lake Erie and long days outdoors alone in the woods and creeks. Civilized human society was more difficult. She studied physics hoping to understand the universe, then psychotherapy to understand humans, then Buddhism to free herself, all while voraciously reading in history, anthropology, archaeology, political science, philosophy, and spirituality. She joined a series of political movements, finally focused on environment and environmental justice, what would be called deep ecology.

Along the way Shodo started one of the first battered women's shelters, worked as a community organizer in inner-city Cleveland, trained to become a psychotherapist, and explored spirituality including Sufism, Dianic witchcraft, and shamanism, practiced nonviolent social change, and finally entered the practice of Zen Buddhism, which unlocked her internal cage. Shodo has two children and four young-adult grandchildren. She has practiced Zen for over forty years and taught for twelve. She still works part time as a psychotherapist.

Shodo's written work includes *Take Up Your Life: Making Spirituality Work in the Real World* (Tuttle, 1996), editing Shohaku Okumuras *The Mountains and Waters Sutra: A Practitioners Guide to Dogens "Sansuikyo"* (Wisdom, 2018), numerous essays in anthologies, and an ongoing monthly blog.

Shodo's ordination name means "right way" or "true path." That path integrates activism with spiritual practice and deeply nourishing engagement with the earth. Shodo has participated in long retreats, public sitting meditation as activism, and walking hundreds of miles, including leading the 2013 Compassionate Earth Walk along the planned northern route of the KXL pipeline. Mountains and Waters Alliance expresses her vision of humans working with the beyond-human world to heal and regenerate life on earth. She lives on a small farm which serves as a learning laboratory for growing those relationships, and as a residential community of practice.

ABOUT THE PRESS

Sea Crow Press is committed to amplifying voices that might otherwise go unheard. In a rapidly changing world, we believe the small press plays an essential part in contemporary arts as a community forum, a cultural reservoir, and an agent of change. We are international with a focus on our New England roots. We publish creative nonfiction, literary fiction, and poetry. Our books celebrate our connection to each other and to the natural world with a focus on positive change and great storytelling. We follow a traditional publishing model to create carefully selected and edited books. In turbulent times, we focus on sharing works of beauty that chart a positive course for the future.

NOTES

Prologue

i. https://www.sciencefocus.com/the-human-body/human-microbiome/
"Due to their small size, these organisms make up only about 1-3 per cent of our body mass, but this belies the microbiomes tremendous power and potential. We have around 20-25,000 genes in each of our cells, but the human microbiome potentially holds 500 times more."

As Ed Yong says in the book *I Contain Multitudes*, "The immune system is not innately hardwired to tell the difference between a harmless symbiont and a threatening pathogen... its the microbe that makes that distinction clear."

1. Refusal Is the Foundation of Sorrow

i. Heres a reference to the research of Suzanne Simard, one of the earliest in this field. https://suzannesimard.com/

ii. In Chinese medicine, each bodily organ is related to an emotion, a color, and an element, and they interact with each other. Lung/grief/metal gives rise to kidney/fear/water, which leads to liver/anger/wood, to heart/joy/fire, to spleen/worry/earth and back to grief. During the pandemic we noticed grief and fear. Moving forward in time, we saw more fear (of vaccines, of authoritarian government, and still of illness and death). As I write this in 2024, we experience fear moving into anger, seen most vividly in the Israel-Gaza genocide. An online source for the Chinese medicine reference: https://wenlintan.com/five-elements-relationships/.

iii. Robin Wall Kimmerer, *Braiding Sweetgrass: Indigenous Wisdom, Scientific Knowledge, and the Teachings of Plants* (Milkweed Editions, 2013) pp. 33–36.

iv. "Start with the rising sun and work toward the setting sun, but take only the mature trees, the sick trees, and the trees that have fallen. When you reach the end of the reservation, turn and cut from the setting sun to the rising sun and the trees will last forever." Chief Oshkosh, Menominee Nation
https://www.mtewood.com/

v. Permaculture principles. https://permacultureprinciples.com/.

vi. Daniel Quinn, 1935–2018, wrote a series of books reimagining the meaning and history of western culture, beginning with *Ishmael* (New York: Bantam/Turner, 1992).

vii. Derrick Jensen, *Dreams* (New York: Seven Stories Press, 2011) p. 245.

2. Return

i. All the quotations in this chapter are from Martín Prechtel, *The Smell of Rain on Dust: Grief and Praise* (Berkeley: North Atlantic Books, 2015).

NOTES

3. Getting Real

i. Morris Berman, *Wandering God: A Study in Nomadic Spirituality* (Albany: State University of New York Press, 2000), pp. 229–31.

Interlude: A New Story

i. Ivan Illich, "Storytelling or Myth-Making? Frank Viola and Ivan Illich," Proclamation, Invitation, and Warning, July, 2007, https://procinwarn.com/storytellingmyth-frank-viola-ivan-illich/

4. Ancestors

i. Luther Standing Bear, *Land of the Spotted Eagle* (Lincoln: Bison Books, 2006, first published 1933). The direct quotation can be found in context at https://faculty.washington.edu/timbillo/Readings%20and%20documents/Wilderness/Chief%20Standing%20Bear%202933%20Indian%20Wisdom.pdf, p. 201.
ii. R.B. Lee and I. DeVore (eds.), *Man the Hunter: The First Intensive Survey of a Single, Crucial Stage of Human Development – Man's Once Universal Hunting Way of Life* (Chicago: Aldine, 1968).
iii. Lee and Devore, *op. cit.*, Vladimir Kabo, "The Origins of the Food–Producing Economy," *Current Anthropology,* Vol 26, No. 5 (December, 1985), pp. 601–616 (https://www.jstor.org/stable/2743082), and Charles Mann, *1491: New Revelations of the Americas Before Columbus* (New York: Knopf, 2005).
iv. Graeber and Wengrow, *op. cit.*, pp. 128–30.
v. Examples and references for this entire section are in Appendix 1.
vi. Graeber and Wengrow, *op. cit.*, p. 426.

5. Who We Are Now

i. https://www.smithsonianmag.com/history/the-story-of-the-wwi-christmas-truce-11972213/
ii. Rebecca Solnit, *A Paradise Built in Hell: The Extraordinary Communities That Arise in Disaster* (New York: Viking Penguin, 2009,) p. 2.
iii. Solnit, *op. cit.*, p. 97.

6. Systems

i. The Ladha and Kirk essay can now be found at https://www.filmsforaction.org/articles/seeing-wetiko-on-capitalism-mind-viruses-and-antidotes-for-a-world-in-transition/.
ii. Lamoreux defines Corposystem as the human social system: "Our human naturally evolved corpo-political-economic-military-medical-educational-charitable social system. Two of its sustaining emergent properties are growth and dominational relationships. A third is money." Lynn Lamoreux, *Saving Life* (Bloomington, Indiana: Authorhouse, 2021), p. 261.
iii. https://www.kosmosjournal.org/article/seeing-wetiko-on-capitalism-mind-viruses-and-antidotes-for-a-world-in-transition/.

NOTES

iv. Lynn Lamoreux, personal communication, September 11, 2022.

v. The story of the restoration of wolves to Yellowstone Park can be found in many places including https://www.theguardian.com/environment/2020/jan/25/yellowstone-wolf-project-25th-anniversary.

vi. History of the changing relations of Native tribes with U.S. Government is summarized at https://www.intermountainhistories.org/items/show/344

vii. Lynn Lamoreux, personal communication, 2021.

viii. Apples are a good example. There are supposedly 7,500 apple varieties in the world. Yet once there were 17,000 in the United States alone, eighty percent of them gone now. This happened because of commercialization. Appearance, disease resistance, and storage determine which varieties will be grown, while others remain in home gardens or not at all. But the additional varieties are important reservoirs of genetic material for the survival of the whole species of apple. To begin exploration, check out this article: https://www.epicurious.com/ingredients/history-of-apples. In the Irish Potato Famine a single variety of potato was grown as the key food for an entire people and was wiped out by one blight; we might selfishly want to make sure that doesn't happen to another important food.

ix. Genetically modified organisms

7. Cost-Benefit Analysis

i. Regarding northern Minnesota and the Line 3 controversy, currently both the United States and Minnesota governments support the prioritization of profits over human life, forests, wildlife, rivers and aquifers (even in a drought), treaty obligations, and local economies based on hunting, fishing, farming, and tourism. Before election, both Joseph Biden and Timothy Walz had made statements vigorously affirming their commitment to protecting the environment and stopping climate change. Somehow, their personal cost-benefit analysis seems to have changed. It's possible their other actions might balance this out, beyond my knowledge.

ii. A search for "happiest countries in the world" yields many results including https://www.forbes.com/sites/laurabegleybloom/2024/03/19/ranked-the-20-happiest-countries-in-the-world-in-2024/

iii. Joseph H Guth, "Law for the Ecological Age" (2008) 9:3 VJEL 431-512. The article can be accessed at https://static1.squarespace.com/static/5ad8bb3336099bd6ed7b022a/5b563fd4124f1c89fba029fe/5b563fd8124f1c89fba02b02/1532379096275/VJEL10068.pdf?format=original

iv. The value of a person was usually based on the monetary value of their "services," so children had little or no value, and a wealthy person was always more valuable than a poor person. Forests, rivers, and mountains were considered to have no value of their own, only the potential profit of logging, mining, fishing, or damming them.

9. The Self

i. Ivan Illich, *ABC: The Alphabetization of the Popular Mind* (New York: Vintage Books, 1989), pp. 71–83.

ii. https://en.wikipedia.org/wiki/Rights_of_nature.

iii. Royal Canadian Mounted Police, Canadas national police force

NOTES

10. The Great God Pan Is Not Dead

i. Barbara Ehrenreich, *Dancing in the Streets: A History of Collective Joy* (New York: Macmillan, 2007).

ii. Its well known that the healing practices of the San include trance and firewalking. However, keep in mind that what they value is not the trance but the fact of healing. This distinguishes them from the current focus on the experience of trance.

iii. Campbells comments on the Grateful Dead and Dionysius are recorded at https://www.dead.net/features/blog/documenting-dead-joseph-campbell-and-grateful-dead.

iv. Its a Mexican saying but originated with Greek poet Dinos Christianopoulos, in ΜΙΚΡΑ ΠΟΙΗΜΑΤΑ Τὸ Κομμὶ καὶ τὸ Σαράκι, writing to those who would have erased him as a gay man, https://ashponders.medium.com/on-buried-seeds-abd4d3ebba7a.

11. Trauma Survivors

i. Resmaa Menakems quote is recorded at
https://talkeasypod.com/resmaa-menakem/

ii. The clinical discussion of internal psychological networks in victims is found in the essay by Patti Miller and Phyllis Solon, 2023, "AIR Network Relational Framework,"
https://www.airnetworktraininginstitute.com/therapeutic-relational-stance.

iii. Adam Curtis, 2002 documentary on BBC, *Century of the Self* explores how public relations manipulates the public, turning citizens into consumers and shaping a narcissistic culture easily manipulated by both corporate and political interests, https://www.youtube.com/watch?v=GFwDc17WZ-A.

iv. Examples: Standing Rock, Line 3 indigenous leadership, Thacker Pass, the Wet'-suit'in, Fairy Creek—and those are just a few in North America; the numbers continue to increase.

v. "O almighty God, merciful Father, I, a poor, miserable sinner, confess unto Thee all my sins and iniquities with which I have ever offended Thee and justly deserved Thy temporal and eternal punishment." *The Lutheran Hymnal* (St Louis: Concordia Publishing, 1941), p. 17.

vi. Richard G. Wilkinson and Kate Pickett, *The Spirit Level: Why More Equal Societies Almost Always Do Better* (London: Allan Lane, 2009). The whole book by these epidemiologists is dedicated to exploring the topic.

vii. Jane Jacobs, *The Nature of Economies* (New York: Modern Library, 2000), pp. 54–55.

12. How It Works

i. The Kogi films can currently be found on YouTube. *From the Heart of the World: The Elder Brothers Warning,* https://www.youtube.com/watch?v=YJNpMxhO4Ic.

ii. *Aluna: A Journey to Save the World,* https://www.alunathemovie.com/.

iii. This and following quotations are from https://charleseisenstein.org/essays/aluna-a-message-to-little-brother/.

NOTES

iv. The statement by Oaxaca indigenous people was published here: "Notice to Centers of Investigation and Corporations," *Permaculture Design: Regenerating Life Together*, Tupelo, Mississippi: No. 120, May/Summer, 2021.

v. Keep in mind that it is only recently that biologists in the Amazon realized that ancient Native American settlements were surrounded by high concentrations of productive fruit trees, such as figs, mangos, guavas, etc. These trees were obviously planted by the ancients and constitute a kind of "food forest."

vi. Derrick Jensen, *Truths Among Us: Conversations on Building a New Culture* (Oakland: PM Press, 2011), p. 65.

vii. D.S. Wilson et al., "Generalizing the core design principles for the efficacy of groups," J. Econ. Behav. Organ. (2013), https://www.sciencedirect.com/science/article/abs/pii/S0167268112002697?via%3Dihub, also Ostrom, *Governing the Commons: The Evolution of Institutions for Collective Action* (Cambridge: Cambridge University Press, 1990).

viii. https://www.ars.usda.gov/news-events/news/research-news/2021/targeted-cattle-grazing-quickly-contains-wildfires-in-the-great-basin/

ix. Martín Prechtel, *op. cit.*, p. 324.

x. Here is the website of the Nature Needs Half organization: https://natureneedshalf.org/

xi. Here is the website of the Half-Earth Project: https://www.half-earthproject.org/.

13. Beyond False Hope

i. Bayo Akomolafe, "What Climate Collapse Asks of Us," written for the Emergence Network (his organization), http://www.emergencenetwork.org/whatclimatecollapseasksofus/?fbclid=IwAR11FKXiFj9ZlykoTsiOomacazTDKS2emCpcUr4qJkJ74UlEn30PO9pUqIo#_ftn1.

ii. Rebecca Solnit, *Hope in the Dark: Untold Histories, Wild Possibilities*, third edition, with a new foreword and afterword (Chicago, Haymarket Books, 2016), p. 138.

Interlude: When Everything Is Conscious

i. As I freely use words about being conscious and having consciousness, I refer you to a book exploring the subject in great detail, defining plant intelligence on its own terms rather than anthropomorphizing. Cognition is about relationship and awareness, a verb rather than a noun. Paco Calvo, *Planta Sapiens: The New Science of Plant Intelligence* (New York: Norton, 2022).

III. How Shall We Live in These Times?

i. The hummingbird story, which originated with the Quechua people of Ecuador and Peru, is found in many places and many versions. My version came from a link which is gone; the most similar link is here, and there are several adaptations on YouTube, in children's books, and so forth. Some stories have the "success" ending, others do not. https://sechangersoi.be/EN/5EN-Tales/Humminbird.htm

NOTES

14. Necessity

i. This website tracks Earth Overshoot annually, marking how it changes over the years. https://www.overshootday.org/.

ii. This website tracks earth population. We reached one billion in 1804, two billion in 1927, three billion in 1960, and doubled that in just forty years. https://www.worldometers.info/world-population/world-population-by-year/, April 22, 2023.

iii. Between 1979 and 2018, the top 0.01% of earners saw a 538% increase in their incomes, while the middle 60% increased by 53%—different by literally a factor of ten. The bottom 20% did a little better, gaining 92% in the same forty years, but nowhere near the increase of the top group.

iv. https://www.cfr.org/backgrounder/us-inequality-debate, April 22, 2023. This addresses the inequality question directly, including salaries, income, race and gender matters, influence of tax changes, and readable graphs.

v. This article details the gap between rich and poor in carbon footprint, and suggests that addressing the wealthy would be the quickest way to cut carbon emissions. https://www.theguardian.com/environment/2022/feb/04/carbon-footprint-gap-between-rich-poor-expanding-study.

vi. William Rees, "Storm Approaching! Overshoot, the Energy Conundrum and Climate Change" lecture at Simon Fraser University, November 27, 2019, https://www.youtube.com/watch?v=VPV7uW7LxFQ.

vii. The literature on all of these is extensive. I will name a few names: Regi Haslett-Marroquin, Peter Bane, Alan Savory, Joel Salatin, Heather Jo Flores, Mark Shepard and a few organizations—Permaculture Institute of North America, Regenerative Agriculture Alliance, Savory Institute—there are many more, but I know these personally.

viii. Personal communication during his presentation on Tree-Range Chickens, c. 2021. He is the founder of the international Regenerative Agriculture Alliance.

15. Nobody But Us

i. Annie Dillard, *Holy the Firm* (New York: Harper and Row, 1977), p. 56.

ii. Consider the deportations to Haiti, MMIW (Missing and Murdered Indigenous Women and Men), and the brutality against protestors at fossil fuel sites. And the anti-voting laws, prohibitions around abortion, attacks on trans people.

iii. Heres a search for protests against lithium mining, which led to many results: https://www.bbc.com/news/articles/cged9qgwrvyo. In Peru, a governor was sentenced to six years in prison for leading anti-mine protests, https://www.mining-technology.com/news/walter-aduviri-peru/

iv. Discussion of lithium mining protests in Africa, https://www.globalwitness.org/en/campaigns/natural-resource-governance/lithium-rush-africa/.

v. Gene Sharp, https://www.aeinstein.org/. Many of his writings are available on this site.

vi. Erica Chenoweth, TEDx Boulder 2013, https://www.youtube.com/watch?v=YJSehRlU34w. Also see books by Chenoweth, especially *Civil Resistance: What Everyone Needs to Know* (Oxford: Oxford University Press, 2021), and Engler & Englers *This Is an Uprising: How Nonviolent Revolt Is Shaping the Twenty-First Century* (New York: Nation Books, 2016)

NOTES

vii. Thomas Linzey and Anneke Campbell, *We the People: Stories from the Community Rights Movement in the United States* (Oakland: PM Press, 2016), pp. 123–76.

viii. Personal recollection with Paul Cienfuegos, on Zoom, sometime in 2023.

16. Finding the Will

i. I learned this in an intensive workshop with Lynn Woodland, who is now at https://lynnwoodland.com/.

ii. Richard Valasek, "Geomantics" course in Ortho-Bionomy, date unremembered. https://www.atplayinthefield.com is Valaseks writing about this work.

17. Values

i. Derrick Jensen, "Five Questions," https://www.youtube.com/watch?v=hk3Ruw1gRIg.

18. Mending Into Life

i. Forgive me; I know that gold mining is disastrous to both the lands mined and to the people who live there. Davi Kopenawa writes about that in his book *The Falling Sky*. These old-Japan images of gold predate that knowledge.

19. Lived by All Beings

i. Strictly speaking, animism suggests that everything has a spirit or soul. Panpsychism ascribes awareness to matter itself. The difference is slight.

ii. David Abram, *The Spell of the Sensuous: Perception and Language in a More-Than-Human World* (New York, Random House, 1996), pp. 11–16.

iii. David Abram, interviewed by Derrick Jensen, https://wildethics.org/essay/david-abram-interviewed-by-derrick-jensen/.

20. Changing the Structure of Reality

i. Research on homeopathy during the 1918 Spanish flu epidemic is an exception. https://pubmed.ncbi.nlm.nih.gov/25134258/

ii. (Vocabulary.com) "also cavort, frisk, frolic, gambol, lark, lark about, rollick, romp, run around, skylark, sport"

iii. The research is documented in Richard Louvs *Last Child in the Woods: Saving Our Children from Nature-deficit Disorder,* (Chapel Hill: Algonquin Books, 2005).

iv. O. Fred Donaldson, *Playing by Heart: The Vision and Practice of Belonging* (Health Communications, 1993). The whole book is on this subject.

v. Human Microbiome Project Consortium, National Institutes of Health. Published June 14, 2012, in *Nature* and several other journals. Permanent location: https://www.nih.gov/news-events/news-releases/nih-human-microbiome-project-defines-normal-bacterial-makeup-body.

vi. The story of Jacob wrestling with God is found in Genesis 32:22–32.

NOTES

21. Taking Our Places

i. Coleman Barks (tr.), *The Essential Rumi* (New York: HarperCollins, 1995), p. 36.
ii. Paraphrased from Sant Keshavadas, a Hindu saint 1934-97. A. Jones and James D. Ryan, "Sant Keshavadas," *Encyclopedia of Hinduism*, 2007, https://en.dharmape dia.net/wiki/Sant_Keshavadas

Appendix 1: Rewriting a History That Is False

i. Graber and Wengrow, *op. cit.*, p. 110.
ii. Graber and Wengrow, *op. cit.*, p. 73.
iii. Graber and Wengrow, *op. cit.*, pp. 319–20 (South Asia), 355ff (the Americas), 471ff (changes in eighteenth-century indigenous North America from petty kingdoms to republics).
iv. Graber and Wengrow, *op. cit.*, p. 54; the discussion of Kandiarok is pp. 48–56.
v. Graber and Wengrow, *op. cit.*, p. 59–61 on Turgot.
vi. Graber and Wengrow, *op. cit.* Chapter 8 offers a rich exploration of real cities and how some of them differ from our expectations.
vii. Graber and Wengrow, *op. cit.*, p. 319.

Appendix 2: True Reports of What People Are Like

i. Rutger Bregman, *Humankind: A Hopeful History* (New York: Little, Brown and Company, 2019), pp. 180–193. Also https://www.history.com/topics/crime/kitty-genovese.
ii. Bregman, *op. cit.*, pp. 143–47.
iii. Bregman, *op. cit.*, Stanford Prison Experiment, pp. 148–54, British Prison Study pp. 154–57.
iv. Brian Hare and Vanessa Woods, "Survival of the Friendliest," *Scientific American*, August 2020.
        https://brianhare.net/assets/images/articles/SciAmfeatureAug20.pdf.
v. The contact source for this and much more is at Honor the Earth, https://honorearth.org/
vi. Internet links were checked February 28, 2025.

www.ingramcontent.com/pod-product-compliance
Lightning Source LLC
Chambersburg PA
CBHW032021040825
30616CB00001B/2